Contents

1

Interviewer
Responsibility
Benefits
Fairness

A SELF-DEVELOPMENT PROGRAMME

Selection interviewing

THE ESSENTIAL GUIDE TO THINKING AND WORKING SMARTER

David Walker

MARSHALL PUBLISHING • LONDON

A Marshall Edition
Conceived, edited and
designed by
Marshall Editions Ltd
The Orangery
161 New Bond Street
London W1Y 9PA

First published in the UK
in 1998 by
Marshall Publishing Ltd

Copyright © 1998
Marshall Editions
Developments Ltd

ISBN 1-84028-135-9

Series Consultant Editor
Chris Roebuck
Project Editor
Jo Wells at Axis Design
Designer
Sandra Marques at
Axis Design
Indexer
Livia Vass at Axis Design

Art Director
Sean Keogh
Managing Art Editor
Patrick Carpenter
Managing Editor
Clare Currie
Editorial Coordinator
Becca Clunes
Editorial Assistant
Sophie Sandy
Production
Nikki Ingram
Jacket Design
Poppy Jenkins

Originated in Italy by
Articolor
Printed and bound in
France by SIRC

Video Arts quotes extracted from training films:

pp 28 & 59: "It's Your Choice"
pp 42, 52, 57, & 81: "When Can You Start?"

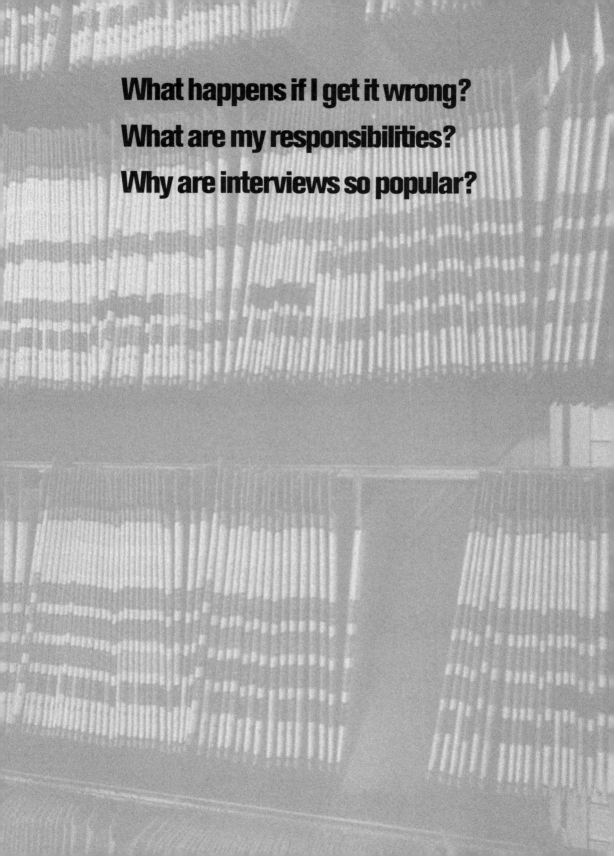

What happens if I get it wrong?

What are my responsibilities?

Why are interviews so popular?

What Is Interviewing All About?

An interview is a conversation with a purpose which is directed by the interviewer towards a defined objective.

This book provides a step-by-step guide on how to plan, prepare and conduct an interview, and how to make the final assessment. It is aimed at the person who has to do selection interviews as part of their management role, perhaps as a regular part of their job, or as a result of having been thrown in at the deep end.

An interview is an artificial situation with an unusual social dynamic between the two parties involved. The people involved have usually never met before, yet they are expected to talk in an open and candid fashion. The outcome is important to both parties involved, but only the interviewer knows the direction that the questions will take and what they are designed to uncover. The power balance appears to be in the interviewer's favour, but the task of carrying out an interview can be a daunting one, especially if it is undertaken without proper training. In fact the candidate has little to lose in an interview and everything to gain, but making a bad choice can cost the organization, and possibly the interviewer, dearly.

Most organizations interview candidates to find the right person to fill a vacant position. There are almost as many reasons why people use interviews as there are methods of interviewing. Often the whole process can go horribly wrong, with the wrong candidate being selected or the post not being filled.

HAVE YOU EVER FOUND YOURSELF IN ONE OF THE FOLLOWING SITUATIONS?

- enjoying the interview but afterwards realizing that you know very little about the candidate's real ability to do the job

- making assumptions about the person and their abilities

- not having enough questions to ask

- being unable to distinguish clearly in your own mind one candidate from another

- thinking they were all pretty useless

- frustrated with this time-consuming process

- unable to decide with certainty who to offer the job

If you recognize any of the experiences in the box on the previous page, you have probably conducted an interview that was not planned and prepared for correctly. You may not know how to. Many people are expected to be involved in the selection of staff. In the past, the Human Resources departments of large organizations have either guided the interview process or taken it over completely. In the modern business world, however, many companies have devolved the interview process down to those directly responsible for the staff. But regrettably, bestowing the title "manager" does not mean that you are instantly experienced and expert in a wide range of people management skills and issues. Interviewing for new staff can be daunting and time-consuming and can easily end up being done badly.

Being able to interview effectively is not a natural or instinctive skill. To do the job well requires the development of an understanding of the process involved and a specific set of skills.

Obtaining information

If at the end of an interview, the interviewer has not succeeded in extracting the necessary information from the interviewee then the interview has been a failure. It is up to the interviewer to get accurate information from the candidate. But do not take all of the answers at face value – remember that the candidates will put the best possible gloss on their answers.

Giving information

The candidate needs to have information about the job and the organization. This information needs to be accurate so that the candidate does not gain a misleading impression of the job role or company.

Interpreting information

The interviewer needs to be able to interpret the information that a candidate supplies during the interview in order to make realistic comparisons between the candidates and to be able to cross check against other information sources, such as test results.

Preparation is essential

The responsibilities that the interviewer has in the selection process are often perceived as arduous but, nevertheless, these responsibilities must be grasped and taken seriously. To fulfil all of his or her responsibilities and to get the most out of the interview process, even before the interviews have begun the interviewer must invest a lot of preparation work and careful thought about the nature of the post that the interview is designed to fill and the type of candidate who will be most suitable.

The Interviewer's Key Responsibilities

As the interviewer the best place to start is to review exactly what your role is in the recruitment procedure and what you will have accomplished at the end of it. You have certain responsibilities:

Planning and preparing thoroughly for the interviews. It is paramount that anyone involved in interviewing candidates is appropriately prepared, understands the objectives and has the skills and abilities to achieve them in a time-efficient and cost-effective manner.

Interpreting information gained from a variety of sources, such as psychometric tests, or other methods of testing where appropriate.

Eliciting information that is comprehensive, relevant and meaningful from candidates. Beforehand get information from other people in the organization in order to determine what you should be looking for in the recruit.

Explaining the relevant job information to the candidate in a clear and unambiguous way.

Awareness that the candidate is often watching you just as closely as you are watching them. Project the right image and impression of the company or organization so the candidate wants to accept a job offer, should you decide to make one.

Meeting the legal obligations placed upon an interviewer, to be fair and not to discriminate.

Interviewing and the law

The interview procedure must be carried out within the bounds of the law. The law protects people from discrimination on grounds of sex, race, creed, disability or marital status. Potential employers and employment agencies must be vigilant about the fairness of interview procedures and selection methods. However, there are some types of job which allow certain requirements to be specified. In certain circumstances (such as in a women's hostel) it is legal for an employer to specify the sex of the candidates that will be considered for a job. You can get advice about how equal opportunities legislation affects the recruitment process from the Equal Opportunities Commission.

Essentially the interviewer must ensure that the questions that are asked and the interpretation of the answer to those questions does not unfairly bias them against a candidate on the grounds of sex, age, race, religion, marital status or disability. Great care must be taken because bias can creep in indirectly.

THE REQUIREMENTS PLACED ON THE INTERVIEWER

The Institute of Personnel and Development in its Code of Professional Conduct in Recruitment states that the interviewer must ensure that:

- the interviewers are fully conversant with job description and person specification applicable to the vacancy

- questions are designed to obtain information for assessing against job-related criteria

- questions which could be construed as discriminatory are avoided and where information is requested for monitoring purposes this has been made clear to the applicant

- the approach to interview structure and content is applied consistently to all candidates interviewed for the specific vacancy

- candidates are kept fully informed of changes in interview times and consideration is given to their time constraints

- applicants are informed of the interview process and test procedures where applicable, the time scale of the recruitment process and the appointment procedure

- applicants are informed of the terms and conditions of employment

- all members of the organization with whom the interviewee may come into contact are fully aware of recruitment procedures and policies.

(Institute of Personnel and Development, 1991)

The Costs Of Getting It Wrong

Interviewing "by the seat of your pants", could have disastrous results, not to mention the financial cost involved. Many interviewers are oblivious to the potential costs involved when selecting new staff (see below).

Extending the process via second or follow-up interviews will also add to the cost. If you get it wrong and the person you selected leaves because "it didn't quite work out..." you will have to go through the process again which will further increase the costs.

An interview is not always a reliable predictor of job performance, but the selection interview is one of the most popular and common methods used by more than 98 percent of businesses as the principal tool for the selection of new staff.

FACTORS THAT INFLUENCE THE REAL COST OF SELECTION INTERVIEWING ARE:

- salary

- number of vacancies at that salary

- how often the job is recruited for

- employer's costs for each new recruit

- the advertisement or agency fees

- cost per hour of the employees involved in the recruitment process

- man hours the recruitment process takes

- new staff induction costs

- training

- time it takes for a new employee to become proficient in the job

Interviews As A Method Of Selection

There are a multitude of reasons why people like to use interviews. An interview gives you an opportunity to meet the candidate and develop a "feel" for the sort of person that they are. You can assess how they would "fit" into the culture of the organization. The questions that are asked also confirm or challenge the initial impression that the interviewer forms of the candidate.

Few people would be prepared to recruit someone without meeting them. Yet most interviewers get it wrong most of the time. This can lead to accepting a candidate who is not the best possible person for the job. If the appointment is not a success the interviewer often blames the candidate for misleading them at interview. Choosing the wrong person can lead to embarrassment and loss of face for the interviewer.

Why bother with interviews?

If interviewing is an expensive and unreliable method of predicting how successfully a candidate will perform once they are in the job, is there any point in bothering? The answer is a resounding "yes". A well structured, well planned interview conducted in an effective and efficient way, will increase the chance of making a successful

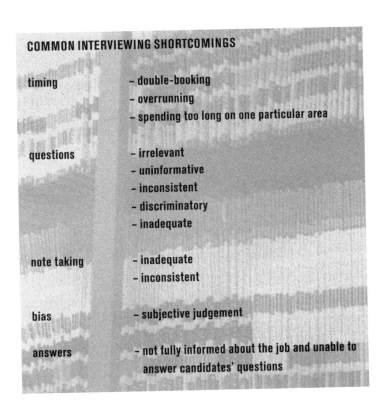

COMMON INTERVIEWING SHORTCOMINGS

timing	– double-booking
	– overrunning
	– spending too long on one particular area
questions	– irrelevant
	– uninformative
	– inconsistent
	– discriminatory
	– inadequate
note taking	– inadequate
	– inconsistent
bias	– subjective judgement
answers	– not fully informed about the job and unable to answer candidates' questions

selection. Research has shown that we can gather sufficient information on which to make balanced and reasoned assessments. The incidence of making mistaken selections and the resulting costs can be reduced.

If you can get it right it should make life much easier, particularly for the candidates whose future careers are in your hands. They will be grateful for receiving an effective interview which gives them the best possible chance.

Interviews As A Method Of Selection

The graph below compares the success of various selection procedures at predicting the performance of candidates in the job.

A score of 1 indicates a perfectly accurate prediction. By structuring an interview you can improve the accuracy of your final choice.

No two interviews are the same

Every interview is different because every candidate is different, even though the fundamental process will be the same. Learn from each interview. Take a few minutes between interviews to decide what went well and what areas could have gone better. For example, did all of your prepared questions elicit the kind of information that you wanted from the interviewee? If not, how could you change the questions? Did the refreshments arrive at a convenient time? Should you break earlier? Do you need to allow more time for the candidate's questions?

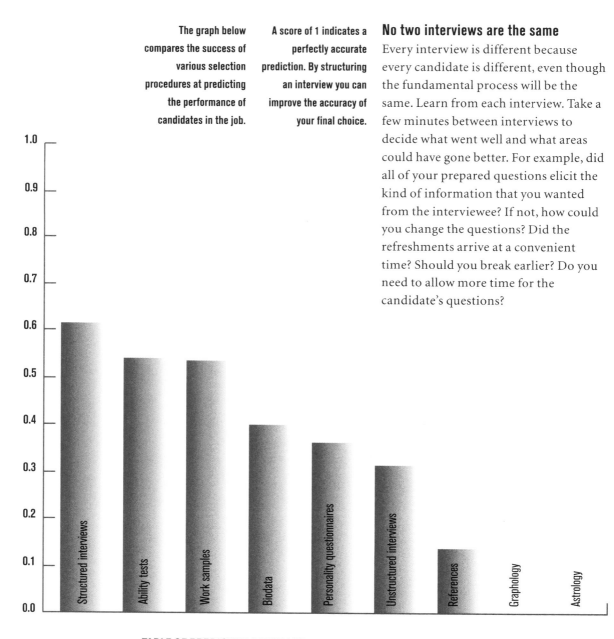

TABLE OF PREDICTIVE ACCURACY

Review the process as a whole

Once a series of interviews is over, look back over the recruitment process as a whole. Your review will probably be more useful if the new staff member has settled in, so that you have an idea of how successful your final choice was. Establish what happened and why. Was the person specification as useful as it could have been? Were there important attributes that you hadn't thought of that affected your final choice? Use this book to plan a strategy for improvement. Any change needs a period of consolidation, so don't change too many things too quickly.

The graph below compares the popularity of the various methods of selection. Interview is chosen by almost 100% of organizations.

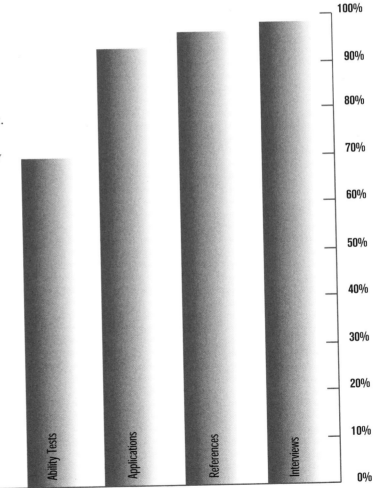

TABLE OF POPULARITY

2

**Self-assessment
Questions
Answers
Scores**

Why Is Self-Assessment Important?

To improve your skills you need to understand how good you already are. A general self-assessment will enable you to identify your strengths and areas that need developing. Then you can plan how to improve. Each assessment focuses on one area of interviewing technique. Choose whichever of the suggested answers best describes what you currently do. But remember that the assessment process will only benefit you if you are honest. It may help you to be more brutal about your current practices if you try to answer the questionnaires quite quickly. At the end of each section analyse your answers and hone your understanding of your own skills.

	Statement	SA	A	D	SD		Statement	SA	A	D	SD
1	I always plan thoroughly					6	It is easier to think of questions once you're with the candidate				
2	There are times when planning is not necessary					7	You can't avoid the odd interruption, after all business must go on				
3	Preparation is the key to success					8	You cannot bring objectivity into a subjective process				
4	You can't plan an interview ahead of seeing the candidate					9	Interview questions should always be developed in advance of the interview				
5	You can't decide what questions to ask until you read the application form					10	Interviews can only ever be subjective				

Planning For Interviews

Planning is possibly the most important phase of the selection process. The work leading up to an interview often begins even before the job has been advertised. It is certainly possible to conduct an interview with no preparation at all, but this "flying by the seat of your pants" approach is unlikely to bring anything more than trouble in the long run. Selection will be hit-and-miss and the candidates will probably feel that they have not had a fair chance.

To assess how well planned your interviews are read the following statements and answer with a tick according to the following scale:
SA = Strongly Agree
A = Agree
D = Disagree
SD = Strongly Disagree
Give your answer to each statement as quickly as possible.

Statement		SA	A	D	SD	Statement		SA	A	D	SD
11	The flow of an interview just happens					16	There is not much that can be prepared before an interview				
12	Good room layout will help improve the interview					17	I never allow interruptions when I'm interviewing				
13	To know about the job, just read the job description					18	I always rely on gut instinct when interviewing				
14	It is essential to start the interview by telling the candidate all about the job and the company					19	Planning the flow of the interview is essential				
15	It helps relax the candidate if the interviewer is prepared					20	I think that room layout is unimportant				

Planning For Interviews

Planning and thorough preparation are vital to the success of any interview. It is a valuable part of the selection process and one that is often neglected. It is crucial that you know whether you need someone to do the job and exactly what the position entails. This will affect how you go about selecting the candidate. For example, it will affect whether you use questions only or some form of testing. You need to decide on the type of questions you should ask and, if you plan to use tests, which ones? The candidate that you are looking for will also affect the application pre-screening process and the criteria for making the final selection.

How will the interview procedure work?

In addition, you need to consider the logistics and costs of the whole process, and the time available. Time spent planning invariably has its rewards in the longer term. You stand more chance of getting the right candidate for the job, which will save time and money in the long run.

Marking your answers

Transfer your answers from the corresponding section of the questionnaire to the grid (right).

20–37

Well Below Average You need to make a great deal of effort to improve the amount and type of planning that you put in before beginning to conduct an interview. Go back through the table and find out what answers gained the best marks. How could you change your practice to match up more to this ideal?

38–46

Fair To Average You need lots of improvement. Note the areas where you scored least well and concentrate on them at first. Take time to think through why your answers might not have been the best ones possible. What do you think you are doing wrong?

47–69

Average To Good You need to improve in some areas.

70–80

Good To Excellent You need to make some minor adjustments to your interview planning techniques.

How Did You Score?

Statement	SA	A	D	SD
1	4	3	2	1
2	1	2	3	4
3	4	3	2	1
4	1	2	3	4
5	4	3	2	1
6	1	2	3	4
7	1	2	3	4
8	1	2	3	4
9	4	3	2	1
10	1	2	3	4
11	1	2	3	4
12	4	3	2	1
13	1	2	3	4
14	1	2	3	4
15	4	3	2	1
16	1	2	3	4
17	4	3	2	1
18	1	2	3	4
19	4	3	2	1
20	1	2	3	4

Imagine being a candidate at an interview where the interviewer is under-prepared, unable to answer some of your basic questions, and has blundered through aspects of what the job really involves! The impression that an interview of this type would leave would be negative not just of the interviewer, but of the organization as a whole.

Communicating With The Candidate

Most communication is carried out face-to-face with other individuals: asking for information, offering advice, your annual performance appraisal, or telling someone what you think of their performance, all tend to be done in a one-to-one situation. This is one of the most critical areas of communication to get right. Good interpersonal communication is essential for any selection interview to be comfortable for

Read the following statements and answer with a tick according to the following scale:
SA = Strongly Agree
A = Agree
D = Disagree
SD = Strongly Disagree
Give your answer to each statement as quickly as possible.

	Statement	SA	A	D	SD		Statement	SA	A	D	SD
1	Communication is a simple process					6	I always make decisions based on what people say				
2	Clothes reflect a person's personality					7	I always understand what people are saying				
3	I can always establish rapport with people easily					8	I never need to check what someone means				
4	People usually communicate better if they are relaxed					9	People always understand what I mean when I speak				
5	I usually know what people are going to say					10	I don't always check what people have said because of embarrassment				

both the candidate and interviewer, and in order for the interview to be a positive and effective exercise. According to research most people are mediocre communicators at best.

Face-to-face communication can be described as the transfer of thoughts, ideas and emotions from one person to another to promote common understanding and action. Communication is a two-way process. As well as getting your own message across

it is also important to listen to and understand what other people have to say – a technique known as "active listening". This will ensure that you can give the candidates the information they want and that you get all of the information you need.

It is equally important that you allow the interviewees to communicate effectively with you, and that you make sure that you communicate effectively with them.

Statement		SA	A	D	SD	Statement		SA	A	D	SD
11	I can always control my emotions					16	Interviews should be carried out in a formal environment				
12	When I hear something negative I never react or show it					17	People who don't talk at the same speed as me can be difficult to deal with				
13	My mind is always receptive to others' views even when they conflict with my own					18	In an interview I always make notes of what the candidate says				
14	I always allow people time to fully present their case					19	I can always rely on my memory				
15	I often show displeasure through my facial expressions					20	People consider me to be a good all-round communicator				

Communicating With The Candidate

DO YOU KNOW:
■ the difference between listening and active listening?
■ how effective a communicator you are?
■ how easy it is to fall into the discrimination trap?

What is the other person really saying?

Your emotions play a large part in determining what is really meant by what someone is saying. The emotions of the person talking will also affect the way that they speak. Without reaching a common understanding you will be left to make your own assumptions about what the candidate really means, which could very well be wrong. It is better to test for common understanding and be certain what is meant.

Both parties involved in the interview have to decide what action will follow. The interviewer must decide "does this candidate have the right qualities for the position I am trying to fill? If so, do we need to take the selection process further with another interview or test, or should I make the offer straight away?"

The candidate must decide "Do I like the image that is being projected of the job and the organization? If I am offered the job, do I want it?"

The environment, how well prepared you are, and how good you are at getting the candidate to relax will influence the way in which communication between you and the candidate will develop.

Transfer your answer from the corresponding section of the questionnaire to the grid (right), circling the number that corresponds with the column in which you answered.

20-37

A Poor Score Concentrate on making major improvements in your communication skills. Pay particular attention to this section in the book. Go back through the table and find out what answers gained the best marks. How could you change your practice to match up more to this ideal?

38-46

Fair To Average You need lots of improvement. Note the areas where you scored least well and concentrate on them at first. Take time to think through why your answers might not have been the best possible. What do you think you are doing wrong?

47-69

Average To Good You need to improve in some areas.

70-80

Good To Excellent You need some minor fine tuning.

How Did You Score?

Statement	SA	A	D	SD
1	1	2	3	4
2	1	2	3	4
3	4	3	2	1
4	4	3	2	1
5	1	2	3	4
6	1	2	3	4
7	1	2	3	4
8	1	2	3	4
9	1	2	3	4
10	4	3	2	1
11	1	2	3	4
12	1	2	3	4
13	4	3	2	1
14	4	3	2	1
15	1	2	3	4
16	1	2	3	4
17	1	2	3	4
18	4	3	2	1
19	1	2	3	4
20	4	3	2	1

Listening Skills

Although listening is one of the most used and most essential of all the communication skills, it is the least taught. This is partly because listening is often confused with hearing. But although most people hear what others are saying, we don't always actively listen. Active listening takes place in your mind (thinking about what is being said), your eyes (picking up the candidate's body language) and the ears (picking up the sounds).

There are many different styles and types of listening, as far as the interview process is concerned. It is important that you recognize when you are not actively listening to what the candidate is saying.

Listen to the tone of voice

The way in which people express things and the tone of voice in which they do so is a vital clue to what the person really means. Use active listening to become aware of the way that people say things

	Statement	SA	A	D	SD		Statement	SA	A	D	SD
1	It is easy to listen to people who are interesting					6	I can hear sounds without being distracted by them				
2	Occasionally my mind wanders when someone else is talking					7	I often make assumptions about what I have just heard				
3	It is necessary to summarize what people have said to ensure full understanding					8	I mentally rephrase what has just been said				
4	I am judgmental about other people's views					9	I find it easy to give the appearance of listening even when I'm not				
5	I concentrate on the speaker's meaning rather than how they look					10	I always look at the person who is speaking				

in the interview. For example, if a job candidate responded to a question with the reply "Yes, I've had some experience of doing that" in a hesitant way, you would probably detect the hesitation and probe further. However, if the answer was given in a confident way most interviewers would probably take it at face value and not probe deeper to find out what the person meant by "some experience". If you don't probe further to find out what lies behind an answer, you

Read the statements in the questionnaire and answer with a tick according to the following scale:
SA = Strongly Agree
A = Agree
D = Disagree
SD = Strongly Disagree
Give your answer to each statement as quickly as possible.

	Statement	SA	A	D	SD		Statement	SA	A	D	SD
11	When asking questions I often use words that the candidate has used					16	I always accept that there are different ways of doing things				
12	I am always interested in what people have to say					17	Listening to how people say things is quite challenging				
13	I always listen without judging other people					18	I am comfortable when there is a prolonged silence				
14	Mentally I would like to challenge some of the things people say					19	I never need to check that I've understood what someone has said				
15	I always adopt neutral body language during interviews					20	Listening is a natural skill				

Listening Skills

...Don't give your opinions, listen to theirs...

will fall into the trap of making wrong or generalized assumptions about what the person has said.

Planning ahead can help you to listen more carefully to what the candidate has to say. If your sequence of questions is not planned in advance, you may fail to understand the significance of the candidate's answers. If you are busy trying to think of what you want to ask next, you will only be half listening to the candidate's answers and you may fail to pick up on key pieces of information.

Stay neutral to keep listening

Sometimes you may find yourself judging the person, or what they have said. If you find that you strongly disagree with an opinion expressed by the candidate, you may find that you stop actively listening to them and instead your mind becomes busy building up your own argument. Most people need to concentrate on developing this area.

Perception affects what you hear

Be aware that your own perceptions can get in the way of accurately receiving the message that the other person is sending. We naturally filter the information that we receive, and this may end up completely distorting the message that the other person was trying to send.

Calculating your score

Transfer your answers from the corresponding section of the questionnaire to the grid opposite. Then calculate your total score.

20–37

Poor Concentrate on making major improvements in your listening skills. Pay particular attention to this section of the book. Go back through the table and the answers and find out which answers gained the best marks. How could you change your own practice to match up more to this ideal?

38–46

Fair To Average You need lots of improvement. Note the areas where you scored least well and concentrate on them at first. Take time to think through why your answers might not have been the best ones possible. What do you think you are doing wrong?

47–69

Average To Good You need to improve your listening skills in some areas.

70–80

Good To Excellent You need to make minor adjustments to your skills.

How Did You Score?

Statement	SA	A	D	SD
1	4	3	2	1
2	1	2	3	4
3	4	3	2	1
4	1	2	3	4
5	4	3	2	1
6	4	3	2	1
7	1	2	3	4
8	1	2	3	4
9	1	2	3	4
10	4	3	2	1
11	4	3	2	1
12	4	3	2	1
13	4	3	2	1
14	4	3	2	1
15	4	3	2	1
16	4	3	2	1
17	4	3	2	1
18	4	3	2	1
19	1	2	3	4
20	1	2	3	4

Avoiding Discrimination

The untrained interviewer can easily become entangled in the area of discrimination during the selection process. For the most part it is lack of understanding, planning and consideration for the candidate that traps the interviewer into behaving in an unfair or discriminatory way. The consequences of making mistakes can be serious, leading to a tribunal hearing.

Everyone deserves a fair chance

Discrimination is a problem for both interviewer and candidate and it can appear to be difficult to avoid and control. If you are to give both yourself and your candidates a fair and equal chance during the selection process, discrimination must be sought out and removed from the interview procedure. Diligence during the job analysis and selection planning stage can help.

Unequal treatment by interviewers can be a source of discrimination during interviews. Selection criteria should be clearly defined rather than couched in vague terms like "smart appearance".

If there is no real justification for the question, don't ask it

Everyone has a different interpretation of what this means. In the absence of clear definitions of what is meant, different interviewers in the same situation will apply differing standards.

To ensure that candidates are given a fair chance, the same questions should be asked to each. If the interviewer asks totally different questions to each candidate how can realistic comparisons be made?

Identify discrimination

In its simplest form, discrimination starts in the mind of the interviewer. How often have you read a person's job application or CV and built up a mental image of the person in your mind, only to find that initial image shattered when you meet them? This is the simplest form of discrimination. The research evidence shows that in these circumstances the interviewer is likely to treat the candidate less favourably than if the person had matched up to or exceeded their expectations.

In another way, many of us can think of people with a certain name and find that, coincidentally, some bad or good experiences have involved people with the same name. This can all lead to accidental discrimination. For example, if you were bullied at school by someone called Chris, then you may find that you automatically have negative feelings about people with the same name, until they "prove themselves" to you. However, you may feel friendly and positive towards someone who shares the same name as your best friend.

How might answers be interpreted?

During the interview be careful not to ask questions that are discriminatory. Certain questions should be avoided, especially those which could result in different interpretations of the same answer from two candidates. For example, it is unacceptable to ask the question "are you thinking of starting a family", even if you ask the question of both the male and female candidates for the job. Your interpretation of the candidates' responses is unlikely to be fair and equal. If on one hand the female candidate answers "yes" the interviewer might think "oh no, if she gets pregnant, she will need maternity leave and we will need a replacement". On the other hand if a male candidate answers "yes", the interviewer often views this as a positive response along the lines of, "good, someone who is prepared to make commitments, take responsibility".

Are tests objective?

The setting of tests, whether psychometric or practical tests, must be relevant to the requirements placed upon the candidates by the job. Badly

Are your questions related to the job and if so how?

thought through tests can be viewed as discriminating against culture or gender. One case brought to tribunal focused on a written test that a bus company had given applicants for the job of bus driver. The company, working on the principle that accident reports might have to be written up by drivers, gave candidates a written test, asking them to write an essay on their hobbies. The tribunal ruled that this discriminated against those whose first language was not English, and questioned whether an essay on hobbies was a fair test of what the company was looking for because accident reports could be dictated if necessary. Besides, was an essay on hobbies an appropriate test to give a bus driver? A scenario based on the facts of an accident, from which a report needed to be written, might not have drawn so much concern. But provision would still have needed to be made for those candidates whose first language was not English. In any case filing accident reports should form less than one percent of the driver's total responsibilities in the course of performing their job, so would placing the emphasis upon this aspect of the job be fully justified?

CHECKLIST
Make sure your selection procedures do not discriminate against people on grounds of:

■ **sex**

■ **disability**

■ **marital status**

■ **race**

■ **religion**

■ **age**

Discrimination Exercise

Remember that employment law never stands still. Tribunal judgements will result in the goal posts changing regularly as new cases create new precedents.

Consider the following example interview questions with a specific job in mind. Think through the implications of each question and the possible answers that a candidate might give. Are the questions gender specific or stereotypical? Could the questions and the interpretation of the answers produce a biased response from the interviewer? If you think that a question would be acceptable, place a tick in the column, if you think that it should be avoided place an "A" in the column. In the other column, indicate whether the question is closed (usually start with can, did, would, will) or open (usually beginning with who, what, where, when, why, how).

	QUESTION	✓ or A	O or C		QUESTION	✓ or A	O or C
1	Where were you born?			8	Do you think that you are capable of performing the assignments of this job safely?		
2	What is your date of birth?			9	Are there any special religious holidays that you observe?		
3	Do you have a family?			10	Have you ever been arrested?		
4	Are you over eighteen?			11	Do you have any criminal convictions?		
5	Are you planning to get married?			12	This job is physically demanding, do you think you will be able to cope with that?		
6	Are you pregnant or thinking of starting a family?						
7	Do you speak any foreign languages?						

Answers

Many questions may appear to be acceptable if they are asked of all candidates. But the problem lies in the interpretation or potential interpretation of the response by the interviewer. In the case of some questions given in the exercise, it might be hard to disprove discrimination.

Question 1

This is an open question with one answer only. It would be relevant for few jobs and could cause discrimination.

Question 2

This is an open question with one answer only. It would be relevant for only a few jobs and could be a source of discrimination.

Question 3

This is a closed question with one answer only. It would be relevant for very few jobs and could be a source of discrimination.

Question 4

This is a closed question with one answer only. It would be relevant for some jobs – such as a bar person – which have a minimum age requirement.

Question 5

This closed question is discriminatory. It is not relevant to the person's ability to do the job.

Question 6

This closed question is blatantly discriminatory and it should never be asked.

Question 7

This is a closed question. If foreign languages are a a relevant skill for the job, this could be a legitimate question.

Question 8

This closed question could only have one answer. It would be relevant for most jobs and would not produce bias.

Question 9

This closed question could only have one answer. It would be relevant for only a few jobs and could cause bias.

Question 10

This is a closed question. Arrest does not necessarily result in conviction so it is not a legitimate question.

Question 11

This is a closed question. A criminal record could be a relevant contra-indicator. It is a legitimate question.

Question 12

This closed question should be avoided as it may lead to unwarranted assumptions.

The Meaning Behind The Words

Be aware that you are a person with your own individual way of interpreting things. This will not necessarily match the interpretation that the candidate or another interviewer will put on the same thing.

For example the way that someone says something can greatly affect the interpretation that you put on it. And the way that you "hear" something may not necessarily match the way the person saying the words means them. So it is important to look at all of the factors that contribute to the message that the candidate is trying to send you.

Read the following sentence, then repeat it again several times either out loud or in your head. Each time you repeat it, place the vocal emphasis on a different word.

"I didn't say he stole the money"

How many different meanings have you managed to come up with? As you strengthened the vocal emphasis on different words, your body language probably instinctively changed to match your voice.

The variation in meaning will be synchronized with your vocal and physical (body language) changes. This exercise demonstrates Mehrabian's theory about the importance of the "three Vs" of face-to-face communication and how they all need to be synchronized in order to achieve 100 percent effective communication.

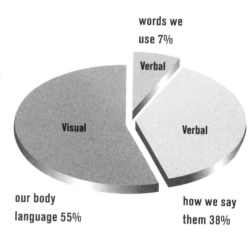

words we use 7%
Verbal

Visual

Verbal

our body language 55%

how we say them 38%

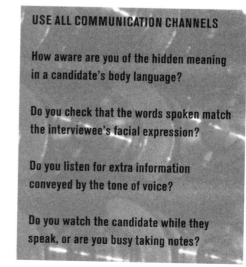

USE ALL COMMUNICATION CHANNELS

How aware are you of the hidden meaning in a candidate's body language?

Do you check that the words spoken match the interviewee's facial expression?

Do you listen for extra information conveyed by the tone of voice?

Do you watch the candidate while they speak, or are you busy taking notes?

Interpretation And Perception

This exercise will help you understand perceptions, as well as practice your questioning and active listening abilities.

Examine the pictures below and write the words that come into your mind to best describe the meaning expressed in the body postures and gestures.

Now ask another person to do the same. Don't give them your answers before they write theirs down. Compare your answers, how similar or different are they?

Analyse the differences and discuss them to try to understand the other person's perception.

Areas That Need To Improve

Based on your scores in the earlier questionnaires and the areas highlighted in the section on discrimination, you should now be formulating some sort of impression of how good your selection interviewing skills are. You may well have had thoughts about other areas associated with the whole recruitment process that you would like to see improved.

Outline the areas that you have identified which need improving based on the following headings, then go through the book highlighting the ways that improvements can be achieved in each area. Alternatively, select a specific area to concentrate on first.

Planning:

Expected outcome from improvement:

Communication:

Expected outcome from improvement:

Listening:

Discrimination:

Expected outcome from improvement:

Expected outcome from improvement:

3

**Recruitment
Screening
Applications
Agencies**

Should I request application forms?

Are CVs easy to pre-screen?

Will using an agency speed things up?

Starting Point: The Exit Interview

During the course of the exit interview it may be possible to find a way to prevent the person who is already in the job from leaving. At the very least by the end of the interview you should fully appreciate why they are leaving the organization.

Once someone decides to leave their job, most organizations dust off the job description and start recruiting, often without fully understanding the post to be filled.

If a vacancy occurs due to a resignation rather than the creation of a new job, the logical starting point is to talk to the person who is leaving. This should happen as soon as possible after the person has tendered their resignation. If the immediate manager has a good working relationship with the person who is leaving then she or he is probably the best person to conduct the exit interview. Otherwise, someone from the human resources department or a manager from another department could do it.

The exit interview aims to establish the underlying reasons why the person is leaving the job. This can often be difficult in the early stages of the interview because the person who is leaving may be reticent. He or she may feel concerned about the impact that their comments could have on future job references, or the remaining time that they spend with the company. This is a particularly delicate situation when personality clashes may be the driving motivation for resignation, so the exit interview needs to be handled with tact and diplomacy. Try to establish a level of trust and open, honest rapport with the person who is leaving and reassure them. Stress that you need their help to understand the reasons for their resignation and to ensure that any problems are resolved.

What does the exit interview achieve?

The aim of the interview is to leave the interviewer with a good understanding of what the job really entails and the problems involved – how the job relates to the organization and other workers. The information gained will enable you to understand what the job involves, the people with whom the job holder interacts, and how it may have changed since the last time anyone was recruited. The information should be detailed and objective if it is to be of any real use.

STEP BY STEP PLANNING SEQUENCE
- conduct exit interview
- talk to others
- decide whether you need to recruit someone to fill the post

YES
- review job description
- create person specification
- decide recruitment method

NO
- end process

CONTINUE YOURSELF
- construct questions
- screen applications
- interview

HIRE AN AGENCY
- hand over job description and person specification to an agency

Step Two: Talk To Other People

The point of view of the person who is leaving the organization will not necessarily provide the most balanced view of what their job was or should be, particularly if they are leaving because they feel dissatisfied or frustrated.

To build up a balanced and rounded view of the position it is vital to cross check the information that you gained in the exit interview by talking to other people in the organization, especially those who do the same or similar work. People who do the same job will be able to give the most accurate description of what the post actually entails. Do this even if you have gained little from the exit interview.

Try to understand how other relevant people in the organization view the job. Find out about the changes that have taken place in the role in the past and ask how they see the job evolving in the future. Perhaps some changes in the structure of the department are due to happen in the future and the post will require the holder to have additional skills. If you are not the line manager who oversees the post, talk to the manager. Get his or her interpretation of the job description. Find out what qualities the manager believes are needed to get the job done well. But do bear in mind that line managers can sometimes have an overview of a job

without necessarily understanding the day-to-day specifics or mechanics of what it takes to do it. The line manager may not even work in the same part of the building, and may only have contact at weekly briefings.

People in other departments may also have something useful to say about the position. Their work may be affected by the job and the job holder. For example, the manager of a warehouse may have daily contact with the company delivery drivers. It may be worthwhile talking to them to find out what type of interaction happens between these departments. Gain as balanced and rounded a view of the position as possible, seen from as many perspectives as possible. Pay particular attention to how the job may evolve in the future.

After all of your research and talking to the people who are directly affected by the job, you should have built up a comprehensive idea of the job that you are interviewing for, what it entails on a day-to-day basis, and an idea of what qualities it would take for someone to be able to carry it out effectively, now and in the future.

The information that you have gathered should enable you to draw up an accurate job description and person specification and it will help you to compile some probing questions to ask during the interviews.

DO YOU KNOW:

- what the selection process entails?
- what is involved in job analysis and why it should be done?
- who to talk to to build up an accurate job description?
- how to screen application forms and CVs?
- how to structure the interview to maximize efficiency?
- how to develop effective lines of questioning?

Step Three: Review The Job Description

Take a detailed look at the job description. Whilst the detail will vary from organization to organization, it should give an overview of the key elements of the job that is to be performed and include:

- job title
- summary of the job
- key result areas (KRA)
- main responsibilities
- who they report to
- level of authority
- necessary qualifications
- location
- grade
- signature and date

The last item, signature and date, are often missing from many job descriptions. These two items are essential if regular monitoring of job roles is to be undertaken. Who is ultimately responsible for agreeing (signing off) the job description as an accurate reflection of the job? The date tells you how old the job description is.

Cross check with your knowledge

Check the information that you have obtained from the previous stages of the recruitment process against the job description to see if there are any significant areas that need updating or

revising. This process is especially important if the job has evolved over a period of time and has become either more or less demanding. Are the qualifications required still valid as the job stands today? Are there any alternative qualifications that would be acceptable? Are additional qualifications now necessary?

A rigorous review of the job description will enable any necessary modifications to be made, ensuring that the person specification realistically reflects the job. This will prevent the recruit finding that the job is vastly different to what they were expecting. Such a situation could result in a newly appointed member of staff quickly becoming disgruntled and leaving. Either way, it is not good news for the interviewer, the line manager, the team or the organization.

Create a job description

Where no job description exists, this provides an ideal opportunity for one to be created. Not only is it useful for recruitment purposes, but it will also be invaluable for performance appraisals or disciplinary issues. Without a job description, in the event of a dismissal claim, the organization could find itself with an uphill struggle trying to prove what the person's job actually was.

...Does the job still need to be done, and in the same way?...

Step Four: The Person Specification

A person specification defines the skills, abilities, attributes and behaviour that will be required by a successful candidate in order to do the job (as defined by the job description) to a satisfactory standard. It will enable you to look closely at the real skills and qualities required. Avoid assuming that the person you need is a clone of the person who is leaving.

When drafting the person specification, take account of the information gleaned during the exit interview and by talking to other people. Look at how the job has changed over the life of the last job holder, and consider how it is likely to evolve. This will allow you to identify additional skills or aptitudes that will be useful and it will help you to design questions aimed at uncovering the candidates' potential for future training. You do not want a person who can do the job now, but will be unable to cope in 18 months because the job has changed.

There are as many different specifications as there are jobs, but aim to cover the general structure given in the specimen (right) when drawing one up. It gives the minimum criteria to be considered. Other criteria can be added, but exercise caution. Too many criteria could create the impossible task of trying to find a "super-person".

SPECIMEN PERSON SPECIFICATION

Physical attributes
- standard of health
- physique
- appearance

Training and education
- specific training
- educational qualifications
- professional qualifications

Knowledge and experience
- job related knowledge
- technical skills
- depth of experience

Special aptitudes
- additional skills
- languages

Disposition
- initiative
- enthusiasm
- resilience

Interpersonal skills
- communication skills
- rapport building skills

Special circumstances
- travel
- overnight conference stays

The job description details exactly what a job entails. The person specification defines the person who would best be able to do the job.

What Do You Really Need?

When drafting a person specification, define the criteria that will qualify a candidate for the job under two headings – "essential" and "desirable". Essential criteria are those that the candidate must have, whereas the desirable skills are those that would be an added advantage. For example, for an administrator who has to spend a high proportion of the day typing correspondence you would specify keyboard skills as essential, but knowledge of the specific wordprocessing software package that is used in your office as desirable. If both criteria are specified as essential, you may risk narrowing the pool of applicants too far. This could end up with you taking on someone who has knowledge of the wordprocessing package, but who is less proficient in keyboard skills or speed than a candidate who has knowledge of another package. Getting familiar with the type of wordprocessor used in the organization is a minimal requirement in relation to the overall demands of the job. After all, the appointee can probably be trained and it would not be unreasonable to assume that someone with good experience would be able to adapt in a relatively short period of time. You could check this during the interview with appropriate questions.

Contra-Indicators

Things that genuinely disqualify someone from being able to do the job should also be considered when drafting the person specification. For example, there is a minimum age requirement to work behind a public bar. Be aware of the various pieces of employment legislation, especially the acts relating to disability, as well as those that cover the broad area of equal opportunities, such as race and sex discrimination. Any factors which will disqualify a candidate must be fully justifiable and legal.

CHECKLIST

- Be specific. Do not use vague phrases such as "smart appearance".
- Decide what is really essential – everything else becomes desirable.
- Try to take into account how the job will change in the future.
- Decide how you will test the candidate in each area.
- Establish a rating scale for each of the criteria which you choose. This will help you establish what is specifically meant by each. It will also help you or any other interviewer to assess the candidates' responses to questions or other assessment measures. Most important of all, it will be invaluable in the pre-screening of application forms or CVs to determine who to invite for interview and, once interviewed, in gauging the merits of one candidate against another.

The person specification will not itself guarantee good selection, but it will substantially reduce errors in the selection process.

Person Specification Worksheet

	ESSENTIAL	DESIRABLE	CONTRA-INDICATORS
Physical attributes What does the job demand in terms of standard of health, physique, appearance?			
Training/Education What specific qualifications, training or attainments are needed for the job?			
Knowledge/Experience What job related knowledge, technical skills, depth and type of experience are needed to do the job?			
Special Aptitudes What aptitudes would be useful to the job such as creativity, written or verbal expression, computing?			
Disposition Does the post require initiative, enthusiasm?			
Interpersonal skills Are communication skills needed?			
Special Circumstances Does the job require travel or overnight stays?			

Step Five: Begin The Recruitment Process

You have now reached a watershed in the recruitment process – deciding which method of recruitment to adopt in order to fill the vacant position. Two options are available:
■ you can continue the process yourself
■ you can hand over the task to a recruitment agency

The time available to you and the urgency of filling the vacancy will probably affect the decision that you eventually make.

Going it alone

The advantages of choosing to do the recruitment yourself are that you have control and that you know your organization better than an agency. But recruitment is time-consuming.

IF YOU DECIDE TO CARRY OUT THE RECRUITMENT YOURSELF, CONSIDER THE FOLLOWING FACTORS:

■ Where will you advertise the vacancy?

■ Who will draft the job advertisement?

■ What will the candidate application format be?

■ How will the pre-screening of applications take place?

■ Who will write and issue interview letters?

■ Will any testing have to be organized?

■ Who will conduct the interviews, where and when?

■ How will you make the final assessments?

■ How will the induction of the successful candidate(s) take place?

Using an agency

An agency will find candidates to fill your vacancy for a fee. The first thing to remember about agencies is that there are good and bad ones. They are sales-driven operations, and the recruitment consultants are usually paid mostly from commission. This means that the consultants are, to all intents and purposes, salespeople.

Are agencies regulated?

The law has changed and agencies are no longer required to be registered with the Department of Trade and Industry (DTI). Anyone can set up as a recruitment consultant or agency.

Good agencies will do the initial advertising, application sifting and short listing for you. Make sure that the agency follows the job description and person specification that you provide.

What are the advantages?

The agency will do the preliminary work and administration work of finding suitable candidates for the position. You will be left free to get on with your job. Freed from much of the hard work, you should have more time to prepare fully to interview selected candidates and make your final assessment. Provided that you have engaged a good recruitment agency, this can be quite a time saving, which may easily justify the cost of the agency fees when contrasted with the costs of undertaking the recruitment procedures yourself. Professional recruiters are trained to do the task in hand, and they rely on meeting your requirements to stay in business.

Requesting Applications

As the recruiter, you decide on the way that you want people to apply for the job. Don't leave this decision until the last minute. State clearly in the job advertisement how people are to apply. The two main methods are application form or Curriculum Vitae (CV). You may prefer to see CVs in addition to a company application form. If you are requesting CVs, state what type. Which is the best for your particular circumstances depends on several factors and will probably be affected by the job position.

Application form or CV? Which is better? Will a CV give more information? Are application forms quicker and easier to pre-screen? Do application forms contain enough information?

Curriculum Vitae Or Application Form?

THE TWO MAIN TYPES OF CV

In a chronological CV the person's work experience is listed in date order.

In a functional CV the information is written with a specific focus towards the job on offer.

Either type can contain a wealth of information, but it isn't always the information that you need. This makes comparisons between CVs difficult.

There are some problems with Curriculum Vitaes (CVs), notably the lack of control that you have over their content and style. You have no control over whether a candidate's CV will give you the information you need. Some CVs are so over the top that they find their way to the bin pretty quickly. Others look and read like clones of each other (this is often the case if they have been prepared by commercial CV agencies or compiled using a computer program, packed full of the latest management buzzwords). Beware of the rhetoric, focus on the reality.

However, there are some positive points about applications made by CV. Although their inconsistent style and layout can make pre-screening procedures more time consuming, it could provide additional information about a candidate. For example, for a job such as a designer, it may be helpful to see how the candidates choose to present themselves when given the freedom of submitting a CV. Also, CVs can provide more detailed information than application forms (although this does depend on the design of the application form).

Application forms

Most application forms are badly designed for today's needs. They often provide a mountain of information, but usually 50–60 percent or more of the information is only of any use once you have decided to take the person on. The parts of the application form that should give the initial key information are usually so cramped, that the applicant can hardly fit in anything of value. The result all too often is that you end up getting standard bland information such as that given below.

This layout and style is not uncommon, but it provides little information about what the applicant's current job entails, their depth of knowledge or any indication of how he or she will match up to what you are looking for. What information there is, is

EMPLOYED FROM	TO	NAME AND ADDRESS OF EMPLOYER	POSITION AND JOB RESPONSIBILITIES	REASONS FOR LEAVING
Aug '95	current	Smith & Co Ltd 14 Enterprise Road Milton Keynes	Area Sales Manager Develop accounts/ Manage area budget/ Plan area forecasts	Improve promotion prospects by working for a larger organization

crammed into a tiny box.

Make sure that an application form is designed to give you the information that you need at the time you need it. For example, you can only really find out why someone wants to leave their current job at the interview stage, and sometimes not even then. So this question is probably not really worth having. Also, unless references are to be taken up before interview, there is little point in asking for them on the form.

Design an application form to relate to the job – based on the decisions that you have made about what is needed. The use of a well designed, job specific, application form will be a major benefit to the organization, the potential applicant and those involved in the selection process. If your organization does not have a standard application form, it is well worth creating one. Even if there is already a form in existence, do not just send it out – review it first and make sure that it requests all the information that you need to know from the applicants for this particular vacancy. Base the content of the application form as closely as possible on the person specification that you have already drawn up for the job. If the application form closely matches the person specification, it should act as an effective pre-screening mechanism. Potential candidates who find that they

WHAT ARE THE BENEFITS OF USING AN APPLICATION FORM?

■ standardized format allows quicker pre-screening

■ easier to develop specific or focused questions prior to interview

■ easier to cross-reference during the interview to check for consistency

■ gives the applicant a chance to decide how they match up to the information required

■ acts as a natural pre-screen – some potential applicants will deselect themselves

are unable to answer questions on the form, or that many questions are not relevant to them, are likely to voluntarily remove themselves from the selection process by not sending back the application form. This should reduce the number of applications that you will have to sort through and pre-screen – saving time and money. It should also mean that of the applications which do get completed and returned for consideration, more are fulfilling the basic requirements necessary for the job – so the average quality of the applications should be higher.

The example application form on the next pages shows how a form can be based on the person specification and can be adapted to be more job specific.

Curriculum Vitae Or Application Form?

APPLICATION FOR THE POST OF:	HR Development Manager

PERSONAL DETAILS

FAMILY NAME: **GIVEN NAME(S):**

ADDRESS

POST CODE	HOME TEL	WORK TEL

DO YOU REQUIRE A WORK PERMIT   YES/NO
If yes please submit a photocopy with this application

DO YOU HAVE ANY CRIMINAL CONVICTIONS   YES/NO
If yes please provide full details on a separate sheet of paper and attach to this application in a sealed envelope

EDUCATIONAL ATTAINMENTS

Dates From To	Name of educational establishment	Mode of study Full/part time	Course of study	Qualification and date obtained

EMPLOYMENT RECORD

Please list below the jobs you have held over the past X years, starting with your current or last job and giving the following information

Name and address of employer • Dates you were employed • Job title and a brief description of your main duties and responsibilites, numbers of people directly managed, financial responsibilities and position within the organizational structure • Your main achievements.

If necessary, please continue on an additional piece of paper.

JOB REQUIREMENTS

Please describe briefly how you meet each of the following job requirements – use additional sheets of paper if required.

1. Professional knowledge	
Knowledge of National initiatives (e.g. IIP / NVQs/ competency frameworks)	
Understanding of relationship between employee development and organizational development / need	
Practitioner skills needed to design and deliver development programmes	
2. Management skills	
Team leadership and motivation	
3. Personal skills	
Situations you have found particularly challenging	

PERSONAL STATEMENT

Please give any additional information that you feel will help to match your experience, attainments, skills and abilities to this particular job position. Continue on a separate sheet of paper if required.

DECLARATION

I the undersigned declare that the information contained in this application and given by me, is accurate. I accept that any information given by me that is proven to be deliberately false or misleading will lead to my application being disqualified from the selection process and any job offer from the company being withdrawn.

Signature: **Date:**

Pre-screening Applications

...The type of person you don't want is as important as the type of person you do want...

Once the job has been promoted or advertised, the applications will start to arrive. The volume, to a large extent, will depend on where the job was advertised and the nature and appeal of the job. Pre-screening is an integral part of the whole process. You don't want to dismiss potentially good candidates too prematurely. Equally, you don't want to be wasting time interviewing people who are obviously wrong for the position.

Sort through the applications and reject those which are obviously unsuitable for the post. After studying the application form or CV closely, you should be able to assess how each applicant matches up to the qualities needed for the job. Start to apply some grading criteria, based upon the job description and person specification to the remaining applications. Assess each application using the following scale.

1 **Falls short of minimum criteria**

2 **Meets the criteria**

3 **Meets and exceeds the criteria**

THINGS TO LOOK OUT FOR IN APPLICATIONS

■ Evidence of skills, abilities and achievements that match the criteria that have been specified as essential for the job as closely as possible

■ Consistency of employment – check that the dates given on the application form or CV match up. Are there any unexplained gaps? If so, make sure that you find out what the candidate was doing between these dates

■ Qualifications compatible with the dates given?

■ Evidence of career development?

■ Evidence of industry knowledge?

■ Stability of employment within the industry?

■ Previous employers

■ General employment stability – average period in any one job

Comparing applications

Once all of the applications have been carefully scrutinized and graded, the results can then be transferred onto a comparison matrix such as the one shown below.

Once the matrix has been completed, it should be a relatively easy process to identify the applicants who you want to invite for an interview, those that go onto a reserve list and those to whom you will send a rejection letter.

It is unlikely that you will find a candidate who scores 2 or 3 in all of the categories, so you must decide on what is more important to the job and to the organization as a whole.

For example, you might be prepared to take on a graduate who has limited experience or industry knowledge so that you can train them up to your standards, rather than trying to convert someone who is used to another organization's methods. However, if you don't have the time or facilities to train someone, then experience will probably assume a higher significance in the selection procedure.

From your assessment classify the applications into 3 distinct groups:
Definite candidates (to be invited for interview)
Possible interviewees (subject to how many of group 1 agree to an interview)
Immediate rejection (fall too short of minimum criteria)

		PHYSICAL ATTRIBUTES			TRAINING EDUCATION			KNOWLEDGE EXPERIENCE			SPECIAL APTITUDES			DISPOSITION			SPECIAL CIRC'S		
	APPLICANT	1	2	3	1	2	3	1	2	3	1	2	3	1	2	3	1	2	3
1	Smith, Jane			✔		✔		✔				✔			✔				✔
2																			
3																			
4																			
5																			
6																			
7																			
8																			
9																			
10																			
11																			

4

Communication
Questioning
Preparation
Structure

How can I build rapport ?

How should I structure the interview?

Should I take notes during the interview?

Preparing For The Interview

The interview must take place in a setting that suits both the interviewer and the candidates. It is your responsibility to make sure that the best possible environment is created for the interview. It should not be a trial by ordeal. You should be trying to help the candidates. In order to help them to concentrate and to answer your questions as best they can, ensure that there are no distractions.

Is the interview room suitable?

The room where the interview takes place can be a great source of distraction. If the interview is conducted in your own office, with your personality firmly stamped upon it (you may have family pictures and souvenirs on the desk for example) this may increase the nerves and discomfort of the candidates. The interview is obviously being conducted on your "home territory". Although a bare cold room can make the interviewees feel ill at ease, too much eye-catching detail can also be off-putting. Have a look at the room that you are planning to use for the interviews. Perhaps you could make some changes to make it more neutral, yet comfortable.

Think about lighting

Pay attention to the lighting in the interview room. You do not want the candidates to feel that they are being subjected to an interrogation. Avoid glaring lights, lamps or even sunlight shining into either the interviewer or interviewee's eyes. If you sit in front of a window with the interviewee facing you, he or she will be unable to see your face properly which will probably make them feel uncomfortable.

Seating can make a difference

You may find that interviewees are more open and willing to talk to you if you are both "on the same side" – literally. Is a desk really necessary between you? Make sure that the chairs are comfortable.

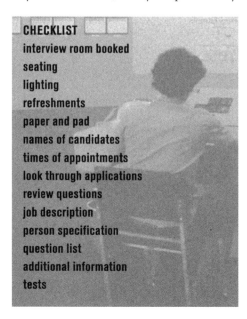

CHECKLIST
interview room booked
seating
lighting
refreshments
paper and pad
names of candidates
times of appointments
look through applications
review questions
job description
person specification
question list
additional information
tests

Do you have everything that you will need during the interview?

Check that you have all the equipment you will need and that it all works. You will need paper and pen to take notes. Perhaps you will need booklets about the organization. If you have prepared an information pack for the interviewees, make sure that you have it to hand and that you have your own copy so that you are able to answer any questions. Have the correct interviewee's application, the job description and the person specification at hand to refer to during the interview. Also make sure that your list of questions is within sight and easy reach. If you are planning to administer any kind of test, do you have the equipment that you need? If you plan to offer refreshments, such as tea and coffee, make sure that you have either arranged for it to be brought, or that it is in place in the interview room.

Know your candidate

You have a responsibility to know who you are about to talk to. You will be unable to ask meaningful questions and will run the risk of embarrassment if you do not quickly review each candidate's application five minutes or so before the interview. For example, if the applicant has stated clearly on their application that they have no secretarial skills and

you ask them what their typing speed is, it will be you who looks foolish. It will also be obvious to the candidate that you do not know anything about them and it will give the message that you could not be bothered to read their application. The atmosphere that this creates will not be one of mutual respect and trust, and under these circumstances you are unlikely to get the best information from the interviewee.

Meeting and greeting

The first impression you make with the interviewee is just as important as the impression that you get of them. In the first few minutes you are setting up a relationship. Always introduce yourself first, explaining who you are. For example, "Hello, my name is Jenny, I am the product manager and I will be interviewing you today."

If you tend to be nervous about meeting new people, it will help to be clear in your mind beforehand about what you will say. Rehearsing what you will say will help you to get over the difficult first few seconds. Don't forget to thank the candidate for coming. This sends the message that you are pleased that they are there and creates the impression of a more equal power balance, which will help to set the candidate at ease.

...Prepare an interview plan and follow it...

Asking Questions

Asking questions is a crucial part of the interview process, but not many interviewers are very good at it. Good quality questions are essential in order to extract as much information as possible about the candidate's skills, qualities, attributes, aptitudes and abilities. Without this information, how can you make good decisions about the candidate's suitability for the job?

What questions should I ask?

It is essential for the success of the interview that you have an adequate supply of planned and prepared questions. They should be designed to help you to uncover the information that you require and to allow the candidate to demonstrate fully their skills, ability, knowledge and suitability.

In the initial stages of planning, work out some job-specific questions that will enable you to establish how closely the candidates match up to the criteria established in the person specification.

Questions specifically about the candidate and related to their application or CV can be asked once you have received this information. But avoid questions that have no direct relevance to the job or which cannot be shown to be directly relevant to the job.

TYPE	USE	EXAMPLE
Open Often contain "who, what, where, when, why, how"	Gets the candidate talking openly about a topic and established facts	How would you deal with a difficult colleague?
Closed Often start with "can, did, would, will"	Finds out specific facts or gains commitment or confirmation	Can you use a wordprocessor?
Leading The answer is usually part of the question	Obtains a desired answer. Not an effective interview question type	I suppose in your job you have to be very organized?
Probing Asks for more detail	Tests the depth of the candidate's knowledge	What were your feelings about that?

Questions of a personal nature fall into this category. For example:

"Are you married or thinking of getting married?"

"Do you think someone with your accent would be easily understood by the rest of the team?"

"I suppose with a young family you will often need time off?"

Questions such as these, regardless of whether they are asked of all candidates, are sexist and discriminatory. The real problem lies in how the answers may be interpreted. Do not ask any questions of a personal nature that are not directly relevant to the job.

Structure the questions

Structuring the question is important. If questions are asked in a disjointed sequence, the candidate can become tense, confused or bored.

Group the questions, so that those on the same theme are asked at the same time. For instance, you might have a series of questions about the candidate's skills when dealing with other people, a series on technical skills and so on. This will enable you to structure the questions in a logical way, which will help the candidate to relax during the interview. If the questions are asked in a logical sequence, frequently the

...A selection interview is detective work...

TYPE	USE	EXAMPLE
Hypothetical A question about something that has not actually happened	Tests out possible reactions in specific situations. Can be used where work experience is limited	If you had to deal with an aggressive customer, what would you do?
Behavioural Asks how someone behaved in a situation	What someone did in situations, which may give an idea of future behaviour	Tell me about when you had to motivate your team. How did you go about it?
Reflective Reviews what has been said	Enables you to check your understanding	Does what you have said mean that your knowledge is limited?
Multiple Several questions joined together	Never use this type of question, it is impossible to answer	What aspects of your job do you like most and why? How could it be improved?

Asking Questions

Ensure that you do not supply too much information too early. If you do, the candidate will simply feed it back to you and you will learn nothing about them.

candidate will start to anticipate the next question and continue to give information with the minimum of prompting. Even if the candidate starts to move into areas that are a few jumps ahead on your list of questions, this doesn't matter. Use the prepared list of questions as a guide, not a straight jacket. If questions remain unasked, referring back to them later in the interview can have the dual advantages of helping you to check your understanding of some of the earlier answers, and giving you a chance to probe more deeply into information provided.

It is often a good idea to preface a question with the context so the candidate knows what you are trying to find out. For example, if you ask, "Tell me about a time when you had to discipline a team member. What did you do?", the preliminary sentence puts the question firmly into context. The second sentence asks the candidate exactly what you want to know. This open question format enables the candidate to tell you in detail how they dealt with the situation and gives them the chance to give you any extra information related to such matters that they feel is relevant.

In designing questions, be aware of what you would like the candidate to cover in the answer. Questions should be directly linked to the criteria identified in the person specification. In the

example question (previous page) you may want to hear how the candidate approached the situation in terms of:

- was evidence collected?
- did the applicant give the person an opportunity to explain?
- was the impact on other people discussed?
- was a commitment to improvement agreed?
- were time-scales agreed?
- was an appropriate environment for the disciplinary action chosen?

If you do not get all of the information that you want, you may need to probe a little further. You may like to ask the candidate whether they would do anything differently with hindsight.

Balance the responses

If you are getting positive and full responses to your questions, but it is a rather one-sided view, rephrase the questions to try to balance this. Ask about times when the candidate didn't handle situations well. This will make sure that the candidate is being realistic. We all make mistakes, what is important is what we learned from the experience.

A good selection of prepared questions will help you to listen actively to the answers instead of half listening because you are trying to think up the next question. It will also make note taking easier.

Dealing With An Unsuitable Candidate

The candidates must leave with a good impression of the organization. The interview is a two-way matching process. You may have got the information you need, but if the candidate is not impressed with you, no matter how good you think they might be for the job, they will not want to accept it if it is offered.

Good public relations is always a worthwhile investment, even if the candidate you are interviewing is obviously unsuitable for the position. If after a reasonable number of well constructed, but specific questions, you have a firm impression that this candidate will not be suitable for the job, you may decide to draw the interview to a conclusion. Ending the interview at this stage needs to be handled very carefully, especially if the candidate has not already realized that they are not suitable for the job. Draw the interview to a close by asking the candidate whether they have any specific questions other than the usual queries regarding the terms and conditions.

If questions start to focus on information that can be presented in writing, refer them to the information pack which you should have ready for candidates to take away with them. If there are no further questions, present the candidate with the information pack, tell him or her how quickly they are likely to hear the result of their interview and thank them for coming. It is essential that this step is not hurried unnecessarily. All candidates who attend must leave with a positive and constructive feeling about the interviewer and the organization.

If the candidate is obviously aware that they are not suited to the job, and show signs of wanting to terminate the interview, try to ensure that they have derived some benefit from attending. Aim for the unsuccesful candidate to leave with as positive an attitude about themselves and your company as possible. Although this particular job may have been unsuitable, it is always possible that another position may come up in the future that could be perfect for them. If appropriate, it may be worthwhile letting an unsuccessful candidate know that should a more suitable vacancy arise in the future, they should feel free to apply.

Remember that you should be as polite and courteous to a candidate who comes for a job interview as you would be to a potential client. After all that is exactly what today's interviewees could be tomorrow.

Make the right impression even with the wrong candidate

Active Listening

Some of the active listening skills can be summarized as follows:

L – look interested
I – inquire
S – stay on target
T – test understanding
E – evaluate the message
N – neutralize your feelings

Clearly, in an interview situation you will use a mixture of different types of questions. What is important is that you use the right ones at the right time to gain the information you need. Questioning is a skill that needs practice and attention to detail when constructing the question. If the question is too vague, you risk getting an equally vague answer or limited information. Of course the most important part of asking questions is listening to the answers.

Active Listening

Listening is a skill taken for granted, often because it is confused with hearing. Listening, however, involves not only the sense of hearing, but also active techniques and skills which demonstrate that listening is taking place.

EFFECTIVE LISTENING

THE VERBAL SKILLS
ASK QUESTIONS
- to seek clarification
- to get further information
- to probe deeper
- use open questions (who, what, where, when, why, how, which)

MAKE RESPONSES
- supportive and encouraging noises or words
- inputs which summarize or build on what is said and take it further
- points that challenge ideas put forward in the context given

NON-VERBAL SKILLS
MAKE SUPPORTIVE GESTURES:
- nod
- smile

TAKE NOTES
- jot down key words
- use the notes for later questions

LOOK INTERESTED
- make eye contact, but do not stare
- face the candidate
- lean forward slightly where appropriate
- friendly facial expression
- relaxed, calm and not fidgeting

NOTE WHAT IS NOT SAID
- listen between the lines
- listen to vocal inflection

GENERAL TECHNIQUES

OBSERVE THE CANDIDATE
- what are their feelings?
- do they believe in what they are saying?

STAY NEUTRAL
- do not allow your emotional responses to inhibit your listening
- encourage the candidate to continue

TEST YOUR UNDERSTANDING
- make sure that your interpretation is correct
- check meaning of jargon terms

EVALUATE THE MESSAGE
- pick out the key points
- think about the meaning of what the candidate is saying

SUMMARIZE
- bring points together
- check interpretation
- allow the candidate to question or clarify points

BARRIERS TO EFFECTIVE LISTENING

VERBAL BARRIERS
- interrupting the speaker
- nit-picking and getting bogged down in detail over trivial points of fact or interpretation
- talking to another person
- letting arguments and emotive responses get in the way
- asking closed questions inhibits the flow of things
- asking questions about another subject
- changing the subject

NON-VERBAL BARRIERS
- avoiding eye contact, yawning
- fiddling, fidgeting and constantly changing seating position
- clock watching
- tidying papers, rearranging notes
- inattention, looking elsewhere
- being distracted

BAD LISTENING TECHNIQUES
- trying to look interested when you are not
- becoming engrossed in one particular aspect
- getting emotionally involved and defensive
- being distracted by other sights or sounds, such as the candidate's accent, repetitive use of words, or the colour of clothing
- switching off due to lack of understanding or the perceived difficulty of a subject
- selective listening – listening only for facts or ideas that you agree with

Building Rapport

Rapport is essential. If the candidate is relaxed, the flow of conversation between you will be more effective and informative. This will not be achieved by simply asking the candidate how their journey was. However, rapport is much more than just a few simple basic questions. Building rapport with the candidate is about "sameness" and the flexibility of the interviewer to be able to communicate in a similar way, to enhance the conversational flow during the course of the interview. The more relaxed the candidate is, the easier the flow of the interview. A good rapport will produce an interview that is more like a conversation than an interrogation.

We all communicate in slightly different ways so it is important that you recognize your own preferred communications style and learn to recognize and identify the styles of others. The advantage of being able to do this is that you will be able to maximize the time spent asking the candidate questions.

We all receive and internalize information from the outside world via the five senses: sight, sound, feel (which includes emotion in this case), smell, and taste. During face-to-face communication you will mainly use sight, sound and feel. How a person communicates depends upon their "lead sensory system" – the sense that is used to access past experiences from the person's memory.

Behavioural clues should be able to help you to identify a candidate's preferred style of communication. The objective of this recognition is not to stereotype the other person, but to enable you to identify how the candidate might be thinking. The clues will come from the consistent language patterns that the person uses, their eye movements, voice qualities, breathing patterns and gestures.

Visual Preference

People with a preference for visually based communication think in pictures. Memories are often vivid with pictorial detail, but associated sounds and feelings are not so intense. When recalling memories they describe how things looked rather than what was said, or how they may have felt at that time. When it comes to ideas, someone with a visual preference will tend to be conceptual and big picture oriented, rather than focusing on details.

The words that they use and their language patterns will give strong clues as to their preference. Much of their language will contain visually based words and phrases, such as:

"that looks good"

"I get the picture"

"that's one way of looking at it"

"let's focus on this"

When people talk, their eyes move around – up, down, side to side, fixed gaze and many other combinations. Research has shown that eye movements correspond with how we access and process information. Those with a visual preference will look up to their right when constructing information, and up to their left when recalling information or past experiences.

If we observe the breathing behaviour of a person with a preference for a visual communication style, their breathing is often shallow and faster than that of people who communicate with other styles. Gestures can be exaggerated and they are usually in an upward direction. For example, the fingers may point upwards or form a steeple when the person is thinking. Because they are often trying to keep up with their mental images, their voice has a tendency to be fast, often slightly raised in pitch, when compared to those with an auditory or kinesthetic communication preference.

Auditory Preference

People with an auditory communication preference make distinctions with sound rather than pictures or feelings. Often they can recall exact words and phrases used by others in meetings or conversations, but may have limited recall of the surroundings at the time of the meeting or conversation. They may be unable to recall exactly how they felt at the time. People with an auditory preference are more likely to recall the vocal characteristics of who was speaking, or any background noises.

The words that are used and language patterns, give strong clues as to their preference. Much of their language will contain auditory based words and phrases, such as:

"I hear what you're saying"

"that rings a bell"

"talk me through it"

"in a manner of speaking"

"I distinctly remember them saying"

"that sounds like a winner"

If you give a person with an auditory preference something to read, such as a report, it is quite possible that you will see their lips move as they read through it. You may even hear them talking their way through it. Once they have finished, they will often say something like, "that sounds okay". In terms of genuine logic, how can something that is written sound okay? This is a clear indication of an auditory preference.

Because people with an auditory preference tend to think in terms of sounds, their eye movements are from side to side as if going from ear to ear. Someone with an auditory preference will look towards their right ear when constructing information or sounds and towards their left ear when recalling information or sounds.

Someone with an auditory preference will have a more full-chested breathing pattern with their head positioned as if listening for something, rather than the shallow breathing of someone with a visual preference. Frequent touching of the ears, rhythmical body movements such as swaying, especially when thinking, and a voice with a good tonal range and resonance, can also indicate an auditory preference.

Kinesthetic Preference

Those people with a kinesthetic communication preference are much more feeling based. They like to get a feel about something rather than hear about it or see a picture. They tend to be detail and logic based, especially when describing something, and will often go into great depth. However, when making decisions or being asked to give a deadline, they will go with what they "feel is right" rather than anything else. The words that they use give strong clues. Much of their language will contain, on a consistent basis, words and phrases, such as:

"how does that feel?"

"can you grasp the idea?"

"let's go through this a step at a time"

"it barely scratches the surface"

"what are the concrete facts?"

"it just doesn't feel right"

"I can't put my finger on it"

"you'll need to dig deeper than that"

Someone with a preference for kinesthetic thought tends to look down to the right when accessing their thoughts. From here they can get in touch with either their internal feelings or externally tactile feelings.

When "kinesthetics" are thinking, their breathing patterns tend to be deeper and more abdominal compared to those of the person with a visual or auditory communication preference. Their gestures are often minimal, perhaps with the head tilted slightly downward. The speech of someone with a kinesthetic preference tends to be slower than that of the "visual" or "auditory". It is usually much more measured and deliberate, with frequent pauses so that they can check how they feel about what they are saying and what they might say next.

Inner Dialogue

Having a chat with yourself while you think is something that everyone does. The internal conversation is often a way of cross checking the information created visually, auditorially or kinesthetically.

During a conversation, if you watch the other person's eyes, they often move briefly down to the left. The "visual" will be questioning "is that really the correct picture?". The "auditory" will be wondering, "was that really what was said?". The "kinesthetic" will be questioning their feelings about what they have said or are about to say.

There are no right or wrong ways of thinking or processing information and people do not have one preference for communication to the total exclusion of the other types. We are all a mixture of the three styles, visual, auditory and kinesthetic, but research has clearly shown that each person has a preference.

Getting along

Once you become more attuned to other people's communication preferences, rapport building becomes easier. We tend to know when rapport is there and express it through clichés, such as "we're on the same wavelength". Conversation seems to flow and after a short period of time we feel comfortable and "as if we have known the other person for ages".

Where there is little or no rapport, this also becomes obvious very quickly. Sometimes you need to accept that you can't like everyone and not everyone will like you. Perhaps this is the time to ask yourself how your communication preference matches the other person's. If they are using a slightly different language pattern to you and their eye movements appear different to yours, then change a few of your words to mirror those used by the other person. For example, instead of saying "how does that look?", you could say "how does that sound?" or "how do you feel about that?". If necessary, slow your speech delivery speed a little and match the breathing rate of the other person for a short time. Major changes to your preferred pattern are unlikely to be sustainable, but they can be made effectively over a short period of time. Notice if changes start to occur with the other person's language preferences and breathing. Almost invariably if you have started to move a little way towards their style, they will often reciprocate without always being consciously aware of what is happening. What you should both start to become aware of is that the conversation starts to flow a little more easily as rapport is built up.

The Interview Structure

There are many different methods and styles of interviewing adopted in the workplace. Whichever method is used, at the end of the day they are all designed to achieve the same objective – to select the ideal candidate after finding out as much as possible about them and their abilities to do the job in question.

Keep to a planned structure. The simpler the structure, the easier it is for the interviewer and interviewee to keep track of what is being covered, and the better the final results. Using a simple model, such as the WASP model (next page) will enable the interviewer to maintain an effective format in all of the interviews.

There are various problems to overcome with any interview structure. Some people believe that a structure that is too rigid detracts from the spontaneity of the interview. This can be true, but a slightly rigid structure is better than conducting a thoroughly ineffective interview. Try to view the structure as a guide rather than a straight jacket. Apply it flexibly using your discretion.

INFORMATION PACK

Most candidates will want to know about terms and conditions of employment. Instead of having to answer the same questions several times, gather the information together in an information pack which can be presented to each candidate after the interview.

DISADVANTAGES OF INTERVIEWING WITHOUT A STRUCTURE

- the approach to the interview is random
- the candidate becomes less responsive and confused
- every interview is different, thus leading to inconsistencies
- assessment between candidates becomes almost impossible
- candidates go away with a poor impression of you and the organization
- risk of falling foul of the legislation that impacts upon the selection process

BENEFITS OF INTERVIEWING WITH A STRUCTURE

- uniformity and consistency across all interviews
- puts the candidates at ease
- a much easier candidate assessment
- a much more professional and detailed interview
- all candidates leave feeling that they have experienced an effective and constructive interview, one that enabled and encouraged them to give of their best

The WASP Structure

Welcome

Ensure that the room layout is conducive to a relaxed but professional interview. Interviews across a desk should be avoided because it often forms an unhelpful barrier between the interviewer and the candidate.

Ensure that reception staff have a list of people who are expected for interviews, the times that they are due and clear instructions on what to do with them as they arrive. Encourage reception staff to use each candidate's name, because this will help to enhance the image of your organization, and it will help to put the candidates at ease.

Consider in some detail how you intend to greet and welcome the candidates. Also confirm the purpose of the interview, giving brief information about the job, together with an outline of the format or agenda for the interview.

Ask

Start asking specific questions. One of the easiest ways to move into this part of the interview is to ask an open question. For instance, asking the candidate to describe, in some detail, their current job and what they actually do. You can then start to ascertain what skills and abilities they are using. If possible, pick up on something that the candidate has mentioned and use that to lead you into the specific questions that you want to ask. Quickly start to establish the skills and abilities that the candidate has and how they can be applied to the job. Interviewers often go back through the candidate's application form and inquire about jobs that they have held in the past. Some even start right from the very beginning of the application form and check the candidate's educational qualifications. Whilst these are important areas to check, they should be avoided as a starting point. Use your discretion as to how appropriate it is to go back over the candidate's earlier jobs and educational history. Refer only to those things which will have an impact on the person specification which you assembled for the job. What is important is how the candidate is applying their skills, abilities and knowledge to their existing job. By asking questions before you supply too much information, you will stay in control of the interview, without dominating it.

Before the interview spend some time working out the principal questions that you want to ask with reference to the person specification. It is essential that you have enough questions, so prepare too many rather than too few. It would be unhelpful to have to end an interview prematurely without having gained enough information. By preparing questions in advance you can use the same set of questions for all candidates, which will make comparisons easier. It will also ensure that the candidates are treated equally and fairly. When planning your questions, anticipate the type of information that each question is designed to uncover and make a note of it. This will help you to take relevant notes during the interview and will act as a prompt to make sure that you extract the maximum relevant information.

Supply

Once you are satisfied that you have sufficient information from the candidate, the supply stage gives them the opportunity to ask questions relating to the job and the company. Many are likely to be standard – queries about terms and conditions, pay, holiday periods and so on. The interviewer should have as much of this information to hand as possible, perhaps in the form of an information pack for the candidate to take away. Check that you have covered the questions to the candidate's satisfaction, especially job-related questions. You don't want the candidate to leave with any misconceptions about the position or organization.

Part

Conclude the interview by carrying out a final summary of the information that you have gained about the candidate. Make sure that your understanding is correct and that no crucial pieces of information have been missed. Go back over your notes and ask questions about the key pieces of relevant information that you have gained so far. As well as correcting any mistakes, this stage can also help the candidate. Hearing your interpretation of what they said can give them the opportunity to add to the information or correct it. The candidate will leave the interview knowing that they have had every opportunity to "sell themselves". This will also confirm to the candidate that you have really listened to them.

Describe the next stage of the selection process and tell the interviewee when they can expect to hear the outcome. If travelling and other expenses are to be reimbursed, this would probably be a convenient point at which to do this.

Remember to thank the candidate for coming to interview and for expressing an interest in the job and your organization. It may seem an obvious piece of advice, but many interviewers forget this basic courtesy.

The WASP model

W – Welcome
A – Ask questions
S – Supply information and allow the candidate to ask questions
P – Part company

Taking Notes

WHY DON'T PEOPLE TAKE NOTES?

I can't listen and take notes at the same time.

If I've got my head down writing, I can't see the candidate's reactions.

It causes a distraction for the candidate, wondering what I'm writing.

Take notes during the interview no matter how good you might think your memory is. Memory can not always be relied on, especially for detail. Imagine interviewing five or six people in a day. Would you honestly be able to differentiate between the candidates' answers to your questions in your memory? Probably not.

Note taking is the only way that you can cross-reference the information that you gathered during the interview process. It is a crucial tool that will help you to differentiate between candidates and compare them once all the interviews are over.

You have a legal duty to keep interview notes for a period of at least six months after the interview, (although in practice it is better to keep them for up to twelve months). If any candidate feels that he or she was treated unfairly at interview, they can then present their case to a tribunal up to three months after the interview and final selection decision. It can take the tribunal a further three months before they notify the company or organization that there is a case to answer. The tribunal will ask for a copy of the interviewer's notes. If you don't have interview notes you may find it difficult to prove that you conducted a fair interview, were consistent with each candidate interviewed and made a reasoned

assessment when making your final selection choice.

Prepare your questions in advance, especially those related to the job. Use this preparation as part of your note-taking process. You should know what information the question is designed to extract from the candidate. List them below the question and tick each piece as it is covered by the candidate's answer. Leave space for additional information that the candidate gives you and use key words or short phrases to note it down. If extra questions arise, either due to something that the candidate said or omitted to say, jot down a few key words to remind you what you asked and why and then link it into the response given by the candidate.

Under a supplementary question column add specific questions that you want to ask the candidate based on information provided in their application form or CV.

Your primary questions should follow on from each other logically. As well as relaxing, the candidate will quite often start to anticipate the next question and continue to provide information. This flowing, more conversational style makes the whole process easier and more comfortable for both the interviewer and the interviewee. A logical sequence of questions will also make the task of taking notes simpler.

TAKING NOTES WILL HELP YOU TO

- summarize more effectively during and at the end of the interview
- ensure that all points are covered
- help ensure consistency of all interviews
- enable better comparison between candidates at the final stage of the process
- meet legal and recruitment codes of good practice

Example note-taking format

Remember to write down the positive and negative things that the candidate tells you, so that you get a balanced picture. Avoid writing immediately after the candidate has said something negative, because this might have the effect of putting the brakes on the flow and may make the candidate less responsive.

PRIMARY QUESTIONS	ANSWERS	SUPPLEMENTARY QUESTIONS

Tell us how you coped with a difficult management issue at work.
 	
    leadership?
    initiative?
    diplomacy?
    knowledge?
	Had to discipline a member of staff for bad time-keeping.
	
	Yes, but I had to update disciplinary procedures in line with current legal requirements.
	
	Not enough warning stages in place.
		Did the company have procedures for you to follow?
		
		What was wrong with them as they stood?

What training courses have you attended that were useful to your job?	I recently completed a six month course on the law and employment.	

5

Comparison
Evidence
Weighting
Tests

How do I choose the right person?

Are there other assessment methods?

How can an evidence matrix help?

How Do I Choose The Right Person?

Do I know how to choose the right person?

What methods can I use to help me?

Can I avoid relying on "gut instinct"?

How can I bring more objectivity into the process?

How do I avoid the personal bias trap?

How to select the right person for the job is probably one of the most frequently asked questions by those involved in the recruitment and selection of staff. Unfortunately, it is one that there is no definitive answer to.

A common problem for interviewers is that after the interviews are over it is difficult to choose between the candidates. Many interviewers throw their hands up in horror and say "they all looked good, it's so difficult to choose". Sometimes second interviews can make the choice easier, partly by narrowing the field. Some candidates will naturally fall by the wayside, having taken up job offers elsewhere or having lost interest (especially if there has been a long time delay). Those that are left can be interviewed a second time, but the quality and depth of questioning is often lacking and no further information or insight is gained. The only thing it does is refresh the interviewer's memory. The outcome all too often is to simply take the person that you liked most – a gut instinct selection. It might turn out to be the right choice, but more often you end up with a reasonable recruit rather than the best recruit.

So what other options are available? In the initial planning stage you identified the elements of the job that were important and then established the criteria against which you would measure all candidates – the person specification. Matching candidates against these criteria happens mainly via the questions asked at the interview. If other types of testing were carried out, you will also have the scores or ratings from these. You have been collecting large amounts of evidence which will allow you to judge each candidate against what is needed to do the job effectively and quickly.

There are almost as many different ways of collating the information as there are decision-making strategies. Stick to a simple method such as the one shown on the next page; over complication can lead to confusion and the wrong decision being made.

DON'T RELY ON GUT FEELING

- choosing the wrong person for the job because of relying on your instincts could backfire
- people who have to work with the person who you select will not be contented with a second choice colleague
- if the person you choose is not right for the job, they too will become dissatisfied and unhappy
- in the selection process you are legally obliged to be fair and non-discriminatory. You must be able to justify your selection with facts – "gut feel" is not good enough

EVIDENCE MATRIX					
CRITERIA	**APP FORM**	**INTERVIEW 1**	**INTERVIEW 2**	**TESTS**	**OTHER**
Proven selling skills					
Presentation abilities					
Rapport building skills					
Industry knowledge					
Team leading skills					
Relevant qualifications					

Example method of evidence collection

You can even add a scoring mechanism to this type of matrix, such as:

✓ knowledge or skill found
✗ knowledge or skill not demonstrated
N neutral – no evidence found
➜ further probing needed to be certain

This matrix shows the criteria needed for the job, the various sources of information – the application form or CV, first interview, second interview (if applicable), test results and other sources). Once a matrix has been completed for each candidate, you should be able to identify the person who most closely matches the requirements for the job. The matrix will also highlight the areas where you have little or no information, which will help you to decide whether or not to bring people back for another interview, and what you need to find out from them if you do. If you have sufficient information to make your selection, it has served its purpose.

Weighting

A useful refinement of the matrix is to apply a weighting scale to those criteria that are considered important for the job. Weight the qualities or skills that are essential, or which form the bulk of the daily tasks, most heavily. Weight the least important parts of the job more lightly. Only include those criteria that can be measured or observed and avoid using those criteria that have already been measured via a selection test (psychometric tests for example).

Assess each candidate on how they rate against each criterion on a scale of 1 to 10. Multiply each score by the weighting factor for that aspect of the job. In theory the candidate with the highest total score should be the best suited for the job.

For example

Criteria	Score	Weighted score
Keyboard skills	7	70

Complete the form from right to left as shown so that after you have assessed candidate 1, you can cover up the ratings whilst you assess candidate 2 and so on. This minimizes the influence of one candidate's ratings on the next one.

Drawbacks

There are, however, drawbacks to using this method. What exactly does a rating of 1 mean in terms of how well someone answers a telephone, for example? Identify exactly how these values are to be determined, otherwise the process will be distorted by the subjective values of the people doing the assessment. The easiest way is to band the ratings. For example 1 and 2 = poor, 3 and 4 = just below standard required. This leaves elements of subjectivity, but it can force you to be more objective when awarding the ratings.

Statistics may hide the true picture. Although one candidate ends up with the highest total, another candidate may be better in important areas. You may opt for a candidate with a lower total score, but a pattern of scoring that matches the job requirements.

This method does not consider how the person will fit into the workplace.

	Weight	Cand 5	Cand 4	Cand 3	Cand 2	Cand 1
Keyboard skills	10					
Telephone skills	9					
Time management	9					
Use of initiative	8					
Organising skills	8					
People skills	8					
Supervision	7					
Delegation	6					
Final Score						
Comments						

Other Assessment Methods

There are a range of other assessment methods and techniques that can be used as part of the selection process. Tests should never be used as the final decider. Any testing should be done before the interview so that the results can be used to bring additional focus to some of the subsequent questioning of the candidate.

Psychometric Testing

Ensure that the area to be tested has been fully identified and is relevant to the requirements for the job.

If personality questionnaires are being used, be clear about what demands of the job will be highlighted. All too often tests and questionnaires are used for no other reason than that the organization has always used them.

Only tests from reputable test publishers should be used. They should be administered and profiled by people who have been properly trained to do so in accordance with the guidelines set by the British Psychological Society. When carrying out recruitment from a large pool of candidates, for example during annual graduate recruitment, consider using a range of different tests. Because standard tests are used by most large employers an applicant may already have completed the same tests several times, which could affect the result.

Assessment Centres (ACs)

Assessment Centres are often used for promotion selection or graduate intake. Using an assessment centre would probably not be a suitable option when trying to fill a position which becomes vacant periodically, but they can be useful if a large number of recruits are needed for a particular job, for example staff for a new call centre.

Most assessment centres include work samples or simulations of the real job. Groups of candidates are put through exercises and tests by trained assessors. Qualities such as leadership, persuasion and interpersonal abilities can be assessed. After a day or two the candidates will have had the chance to demonstrate their skills and abilities in a wide range of areas. The results of the exercises are usually cross referenced to the scores from a battery of psychometric tests. The test results plus the evidence collected by the assessors enable the candidates for the position to be short-listed. The interviews that follow can then be partly focused on the results from the assessment centre, with more targeted and specific questions. This method of assessment can bring higher levels of objectivity into the selection process, provided that it is well designed, but it requires the investment of significant amounts of time and money.

ACs need careful planning to decide what skills and abilities are to be assessed and the best methods of assessment.

Avoiding Bias

Whichever method is chosen, try to be as objective as possible. Remember, some people are good at tests, but not very good at the practical application of many of the areas tested. Other people are excellent at their job, but are not good at tests.

Research evidence shows that there are many types of bias that can influence the interviewer (often without them even realizing it) and therefore the outcome of the interview. Most powerful of all the factors that can influence the interviewer, either positively or negatively, is appearance – that all important "first impression".

Think of times when you have built up a strong mental picture of someone who you often talk to on the telephone, only to be surprised by the real person when you finally meet them. In a similar way when you read a candidate's application form or CV you formulate an impression of what the person might be like. When the candidate turns up for interview, the reality may be disappointing. Even before the interview begins you may be biased in some way.

Names can also have an influence. If a particular name conjures up unpleasant thoughts or associations for you personally, you might make unwarranted assumptions about the candidate as a result.

Perfumes and aftershaves can have a negative effect on an interviewer. If you like a particular fragrance that a candidate is wearing you will tend to treat him or her in a more favourable way than a candidate wearing a fragrance that you dislike.

When interviewing, do not forget that the behaviour of a candidate during the interview is not necessarily an accurate representation of their personality or ordinary behaviour. Behaviour can be modified, adapted or changed according to the circumstances. Personality can not. Do not be tempted to be an amateur psychologist, go with the evidence. You are more likely to get the right person for the job by working with the facts.

Bias can lead to discrimination and poor selection. The golden rule is to "keep an open line". Be aware of your natural tendency to bias and subjective judgement, and use good interviewing techniques to help you control them. The point of the interview is to get the best person for the job, not the person who you like most.

BEING FAIR CHECKLIST

- Adopt the same format and style for every interview for the same job.
- Ignore the views of other interviewers until the process has been completed.
- Maintain a friendly but neutral attitude throughout the interview.
- Let each candidate settle down and relax before posing challenging or critical questions.
- Be aware of your own tendencies to bias, particularly in the first few seconds on the interview.
- Do not show verbal or nonverbal disapproval.
- Ask the same key questions to all candidates.
- Put key questions to all candidates in the same way.
- Ensure that questions are relevant to the job.
- Seek information which is behaviour based.
- Try not to be judgmental about the candidate's answers.
- If in doubt and further questions need be put to the candidate, ask them towards the end of the interview.
- Ask open and behavioural questions.
- Listen to the answers, show interest.
- Check that you have understood the answers correctly.
- Do not interrupt.
- Use the job description and person specification to structure the interview and as criteria for questions asked.
- Give the candidates the opportunity to ask questions.
- Try to get a balanced view of the candidate.

...Measure the candidates against the job – not each other...

Checklist

RECRUITMENT AND SELECTION PROCESS

PLANNING

EXIT INTERVIEW
Conduct an exit interview
Talk to other people about the job role

JOB DESCRIPTION
Cross check all information about the job against the job description
Is the job description up to date?
Do you need to recruit someone?

PERSON SPECIFICATION
Draft person specification
Establish clear criteria
Balance essential and desirable qualities
Determine how you will assess criteria

APPLICATION
What kind of applications? (CV or application forms)
Ensure application form is relevant
Develop method of pre-screening
Get adequate resources in place

SELECTING

APPLICANTS
Arrange for acknowledging
Arrange for sorting through applications
Advise applicants of interview arrangements
Ensure "positive" rejection letters sent out

STRUCTURE
See interview structure (right)

DECIDING
Has assessment of all candidates been fair?
Notify interviewees of decision
Take up references

INDUCTION
Establish induction process
Make arrangements for new person to join company

VALIDATION
Is there a procedure to validate selection against?
Is the new recruit a success?

INTERVIEW STRUCTURE

WELCOME

Set up the interview room correctly

Divert telephone calls

Leave instructions not to be interrupted

Leave a list of expected candidates and their time of arrival/interview with reception

Give clear instructions about what to do with candidates at reception

Make arrangements for expenses to be processed

Work out greeting process and rapport establishment

Tell candidate the interview agenda

Advise candidate that you will be taking notes

Plan primary questions (those essential to job)

Plan candidate specific questions (from the application)

ASK

Plan question sequence

Are you clear about what the questions are designed to reveal?

Have you included open questions?

Do you have all the information that you are likely to need?

SUPPLY

Have you prepared information packs?

Do you know enough to answer the candidate's questions?

Have you fully summarized the information gained to make sure that you understand what the candidate has told you

PART

Tell the candidate what will happen next

Thank the candidate for coming to the interview

Finalize your notes while the information is still fresh in your mind

6

**Development
Identify needs
Action plan
Summary**

Can I develop my skills?

What action can I take now?

What support will I need?

Developing Your Skills

To get maximum benefit from this section of the book it is important to complete all of the exercises in it to enable you to build on the self-assessment that you have already done and to plan how you want to improve your interview skills.

You will identify areas where you should improve your skills, prioritize them and make a personal development plan to help you improve.

Watch yourself in action

The self-assessment questionnaires in chapter two will have given an indication of how good your current skills are. To improve, assess your own performance from day-to-day and week-to-week.

Each time you interview, observe what you do. When the interview is over, take five minutes to record how it went, and evaluate what was good and what could have been done better. It is well worth the time.

Where do you need to improve ?

Draw up a self-assessment table following the example given (right). Transfer the ratings that you got in the self-assessments in chapter two. Be honest when you complete the list.

The exercise will be more accurate if you also get feedback from others – your co-interviewers. It may be worth arranging for a colleague or your boss to sit in on an interview and to give their own assessment of how it went. Ask them if you communicate clearly. Do you ever miss out information or confuse the interviewee? You could also try tape recording interviews to listen to yourself and get a realistic view of how you do. Sometimes things leap out at you from a tape which you would not notice in the real-life situation. Explain why you are doing it and ask the candidate for their permission.

How did you do?

You will probably have identified at least three or four areas where you need to improve your skills; any less than this and either you are an exceptionally good interviewer or perhaps you were not being as honest as you could be. The next step is to produce a specific plan to develop each skill where improvement is necessary. If time permits, try to improve the skills which you classified as "satisfactory". Why be satisfactory when you can be good? Repeat this assessment regularly.

Skills	Good	Satisfactory	Could be better
Preparation for the interview			
Planning questions			
Asking relevant, informative questions			
Note taking			
Building rapport			
Making successful appointments			
Staying neutral			
Fair/unbiased interviewing			
Answering candidate's questions			
Keeping the interview to length			
Making a good impression on all candidates			
Using active listening and questioning to make sure you have understood answers			
Comparing candidates fairly			
Asking questions clearly			
Getting all the information you need			

Preparing To Write A Development Plan

Focus development in areas of weakness that relate to the most important activities. Consider all of the major areas in the interview process and analyse your performance in each. Can you identify areas where you could improve your interview technique? Once you have identified the areas in which you wish to develop your skills, put together a plan for improvement.

First use the model below to consider how you learn. Review your experiences and learn from your assessment. The next step is to plan your development. This should not be a one-off event that you do only while reading this book. To really develop you need to use the learning circle as often as possible.

Briefly review your experiences as they happen and then every six to twelve months, assess yourself and write out a formal development plan for the next period. Use the exercises in the book to help in your self-assessment and development planning regularly throughout your career.

The Johari Window

Self-assessment will help you to discover where your weaknesses lie. A model called the *Johari Window* (opposite page) can help you think about this more clearly. It suggests that there are four areas of information about ourselves and we need to consider all of them to understand how to improve.

THE LEARNING CIRCLE

Having an experience

Planning the next steps
(your development plan)

Reviewing the
experience

Learning from the
experience

Information known to yourself and others This is public knowledge. Perhaps everyone in the office knows that you are the best person at assessing which candidates to invite for interview. Think about why you are the best at particular interview issues. What is it about your personal approach in those situations which helps you to operate more effectively? What do you do that is different to other people?

Information not known to others What things do you alone know about yourself? For example, do you find it difficult to put interviewees at ease?

Information known only to others Find out the things that other people know about you, but you don't know – your own blind spot. For example, have you ever discovered from someone else that you have a habit you were previously unaware of – perhaps you scratch your ear or nose whilst you talk. Discovering your blind spot emphasizes the importance of getting feedback from your boss, your family and friends, staff and colleagues.

Information not known This type of information is the information that no one knows as yet. It can only be revealed through some kind of self-analysis or discovery. For example, in your life have you ever discovered that you are good at something you would never even have thought of? You probably already have some ideas about how you work with people, what you do well and what not so well. Is there a pattern behind this? What jobs don't you enjoy? Why do you dislike them? What can you do to solve the problem? If you feel intimidated by some people, or find yourself having negative feelings towards certain types of candidate, who are they and why do you feel that way? How can you go about solving the problem?

By thinking carefully about these issues you will probably reveal information about yourself which was previously part of the "unknown at present" area. By analysing your problems and trying to find the causes, you will find the answer and be able to tackle them.

JOHARI WINDOW		
Known to You	Public Knowledge	Secret Knowledge
Not Known to You	Own Blind Spot	Unknown at Present
	Known to Other People	Not Known to Other People

Identifying Development Needs

ASK THE FOLLOWING QUESTIONS

Have I identified the areas for development?

Do I know why they need developing?

Do I know how to develop?

By looking back at your answers to the questionnaires in chapter two, identify the areas that you need to improve when interviewing and making successful appointments. Look at the areas where you scored in the bottom or middle of the range and try to assess why your answer was not the best one. Use the information from the self-assessments and what you have read to write what you need to do to improve your performance in the problem areas. For example, if you have identified that you have a problem with greeting candidates and putting them at ease you might write in the space "need to practice what I will say to candidates when they first arrive – perhaps role play with a colleague".

The chart gives an idea of the steps to take to improve your skills. Expand it to give a detailed development action plan.

Interviewing skills area	Things you need to do to improve
Preparing questions in advance	
Writing job descriptions	
Putting together person specification	
Asking clear questions	
Probing for further information	
Putting candidates at ease	
Getting all relevant information from the candidates	
Keeping notes during the interview	
Staying neutral and unbiased	
Comparing candidates after interviews are over	
Making the correct selection from the group	
Altering communication style to match the candidate	
Other Areas	

Development Action Plan

Select the areas where you need to improve and the steps you would take to achieve this and photocopy a Development Action Plan for each.

1. Write what the skill is that you need to improve. This may be "Need to take more care in sticking with planned questions and taking notes – tend to give inconsistent interviews which makes candidates difficult to compare".

2. Outline the steps needed to improve this. For example, "Write out question list and keep it prominently in front of me. Practice with role play – perhaps go on a course".

3. Say whether your boss or organization could help you to improve. If any of the actions you propose would be more effective with support from your boss or the company, include what they could do to help. For example, "discuss with my boss how she may have dealt with a problem similar to the ones that I regularly encounter."

4. Put in a date by when you will have achieved an improvement or will have completed the action that you have set yourself. You must set yourself a deadline and stick to it. If you don't do this, you will suddenly find years have passed, you have done nothing to improve and as a result someone else has been selected for promotion. Remember that it is up to you to develop yourself – no one else will do it, although a good boss may help.

DEVELOPMENT ACTION PLAN

Development need

Actions by:

You   **Your boss/the company**

Organizational support?

To be completed/achieved by

Immediate Action Plan

You may find that the Development Action Plan identifies improvements that will probably take some months to be effective. To keep you motivated in your self-improvement programme, try to achieve something as quickly as possible. For example, "write down main points of answers in bullet points during interview then write up notes as soon as interview is over". This can be implemented straight away. It may help to draw up an Immediate Action Plan – of steps from your Development Action Plan that can be taken at once.

Aim to find at least four improvement actions to take immediately, perhaps including the ones already given in the example. Your interviewing and selection procedure will show an immediate benefit.

Promoting development and flexibility

The workplace is not static and individuals and teams constantly need to develop their skills to meet the challenges of the future. These may be as a result of technological developments, changes in legislation, new systems being introduced, or other factors that demand that the team and individuals within it improve their skills. If people do not share and pass on their skills and knowledge effectively then they will take their expertise and know-how with them when they leave – your company will lose a valuable resource. Try to share your own expertise in interviewing with others and to learn from their experiences too.

	Steps to Take	Notes
1	Develop some stock phrases to use when greeting candidates to put them at their ease.	
2	Set up meeting with my manager to discuss personal development plan to improve my interview skills. Explain the support I would like.	
3		
4		

General Self-Development

To be effective in any job we need to be able to improve and develop our skills. Everyone learns by trial and error or by using knowledge that they have gained from others. Trial and error can be costly in terms of time taken to achieve a successful outcome because mistakes are made and resources wasted. By passing on knowledge these problems can be avoided. Many organizations have found that if everyone can be encouraged to communicate their learning and ideas freely, things get done faster and there are fewer problems. In addition, people develop skills faster which allows more delegation and less "firefighting".

Further self development

You can develop your skills further through on-going self-assessment, feedback from others, training courses and reading other books. Put your ideas and discoveries into practice.

This book is an on-going aid to your development. Do not just leave it on the shelf once you have read it. Go back to it on a regular basis to assess how you have improved and where further progress can be made. Development is not a one-off event. The people who do well are continuously improving their skills.

Role models and mentors

Many people have found that finding a role model or mentor can help them to develop their skills very effectively. A role model is someone whose behaviour you copy because they do what you think are the right things. Your role model may be a successful person whose position you aspire to. Adopting a role model can be an effective tool for self improvement, but there is always a danger of copying poor behaviour. In contrast, a mentor works with you to give you support when you need it and to help you find solutions to your problems. A mentor will be in touch with you and will help you to manage your own development. You can actually access and use the mental assets of a more skilled and experienced person.

Finding a mentor can be one of the most effective of all forms of development, especially when it is combined with self analysis and development planning.

Summary

Selection interviewing requires good planning and skill if it is to be effective. Most businesses and other organizations use interviews as the main method of selecting staff. The cost of getting the process wrong can be significant, wasting time and money and affecting the image of the company.

To select the right candidates you need to know as much as possible about their abilities to perform in the job role. You need to be skilled and proficient in the art of questioning. Ask questions that are constructed to get the maximum amount of relevant information. This will take time to plan what you will ask and why – the interview may be the only method of assessing a candidate's suitability for the job.

Questioning is only one part of the process. Listening to the responses, and understanding what is being said, or not being said, is vital too. Listen to vocal inflection and try to understand the accompanying body language.

Pay attention to how you and candidates communicate. Everyone has a communication style preference. To gain the maximum information the candidate must feel at ease. Aim to establish rapport quickly.

Planning and preparation are essential. Without a detailed job analysis you will not know who you need to recruit, what for, or whether the position needs to be filled at all. To interview effectively you must understand what the job requires. Without a person specification the design of the questions becomes impossible. Know what type of behaviour is needed to do the job well and focus the questions to achieve this.

Adopt a consistent style and approach, so that you can make a fairer comparison between candidates. Make sure that you comply with the legal requirements of the selection process. It is easy to stray inadvertently into the areas of discrimination especially when you are not well prepared. Suppress your instinctive areas of bias by working hard to make yourself aware of what they are.

Take time to analyse what you are comfortable and competent at, and admit to the areas that you need to develop. This will point you in the right direction for improvement, but you need to plan how you will develop and carry out your plan of action. Systematically work on your improvement plan. Review your progress on a regular basis, evaluate its effectiveness, fine tune where appropriate. Avoid the temptation to change too much too quickly. Concentrate on one significant area for action, get it working and feel comfortable about it, then move on to the next, steadily making progress.

You can do it if you really want to. Good luck and successful interviewing.

Index

Taking It Further

Videos

When Can You Start?
Selection Techniques Video Arts
It's Your Choice
Selection Techniques Video Arts
More Than A Gut Feeling
Behavioural Interviewing Melrose

Reading

Anderson, N.R. & Shackleton, V.J.,
Successful Selection Interviewing,
Oxford, Blackwell, (1993)
Bray, T., *The Selection Maze*,
London, Mercury Books, (1991)
Burly-Allen, M., *Listening – The
Forgotten Skill*,
New York, John Wiley & Sons Inc., (1992)
Cooper, D., & Robertson, I.T., *The
Psychology of Personnel Selection*,
London, Routledge, (1995)
Dales, M., *How To Be A Better Interviewer*,
London, Kogan Page, (1996)
Molden, D., *Managing With The Power of
NLP*,
London, Pitman Publishing, (1996)
Pedder, M., Burgoyne, J., & Boydell, T.,
A Manager's Guide To Self-Development,
3rd Edition, Maidenhead, McGraw-
Hill,(1997)
Richardson, J., *The Magic Of Rapport*,
Capitola, California,
Meta Publications, (1987)

Printed and bound by Chorus-France